"Rahanna Bisseret Martinez is a talented cook who is much wiser than her years. She pours her culinary insights into this debut collection of recipes, skillfully guiding and nudging us like a kitchen buddy. Equally important, Rahanna bridges cultures to show us that food is democratic, to be experienced and shared, so that we better understand ourselves and one another."

—ANDREA NGUYEN, James Beard Award–winning author of *The Pho Cookbook* and *Ever-Green Vietnamese*

"Rahanna Bisseret Martinez's deep love for food is palpable right from the very start in her debut book, *Flavor+Us*. As one of the most exciting young cooks of our generation, she brings new flavors and textures to the table in such dishes as Farmers' Market Carbonara, Jerk Eggplant Steaks, and Creole Mushroom Hand Pies."

—ANDY BARAGHANI, author of *The Cook You Want to Be*

"With *Flavor+Us*, Rahanna invites you to the table, teaches you something new, and makes cooking accessible and fun for everyone of all ages."

—CAT CORA, 1st female Iron Chef, 1st female inducted into the Culinary Hall of Fame, and restaurateur

"From the moment that I met Rahanna on *Top Chef Junior*, I knew she'd be a force to be reckoned with. She has taken her love of cooking and educating through food and written a fantastic book full of heart and wisdom. I can't wait to tuck into these recipes with my kids."

—CURTIS STONE, chef/owner of Maude and Gwen

Flavor+Us

Rahanna Bisseret Martinez

PHOTOGRAPHS BY ED ANDERSON

Flavor+Us
Cooking for Everyone

4c
4 COLOR BOOKS
An imprint of **TEN SPEED PRESS**
California | New York

To past, present, and future
Black and Brown girls.

Contents

7

Pantry Basics

Introduction

Cooking and eating—and thinking about cooking and eating—is the Bisseret Martinez way.

The food I grew up with is heavily influenced by the African diaspora and Indigenous Mexican foodways: roasted sweet potatoes with braised greens, fried cornmeal-crusted tofu, and enchiladas in a smoky homemade guajillo sauce. (My Grandma Velia and Grandpa Jean, who represent the Mexican and Haitian sides of my family, respectively, are wizards with vegetables and herbs.) I'm so appreciative of my parents and grandparents for bringing all our heritage to the plate. But even more so, I am grateful they taught me to be curious about heritage beyond my own.

Our family is not composed of boring eaters, cooks, or even grocery shoppers, for that matter! My family goes to the source for all our foodstuffs—Chinese ingredients at the Chinese grocer, Nigerian at the Nigerian grocer, and the same for Filipino, Thai, Korean, Jamaican, Pakistani, Jewish, Italian, Black American, and Arab. This is possible when you live in a city like my hometown, Oakland, which has a diverse population. When I'm grocery shopping, I set aside any shyness, walk up to the people in charge, and ask about all their secrets: the best techniques for preparing their store products, their favorite ingredients, and what is freshest and in season now.

Once, when I was at Mi Pueblo, my source for Mexican ingredients in Oakland, I stood behind a woman in the checkout line and had my eyes set on her basket, which contained only one item: dried shrimp. Piles of it. Hmmm. I knew dried shrimp were used—especially in Asian and African cooking—for stocks, soups, sauces, and more, but this woman seemed to be stocking up for something special. I couldn't stop myself: "Excuse me," I said, pointing to her shrimp stash, "what will you be cooking with those?" She met my gaze and smiled big. Her answer: cucumbers and corn tortilla chips with a Mexican-style hot sauce, her favorite snack. She said, "You know, like nopales." And I knew exactly what she meant, because I had these at many a lunch party and in Mi Pueblo's prepared food area. For this dish, the cactus thorns are carefully removed from the nopales and then the nopales are diced into cubes with tomatoes, cucumbers, and lime juice. Oh! I went home and tried it. The saltiness and tang of the shrimp and hot sauce paired so well with the cool, crisp cucumbers. The toasty tortilla chips brought it all together in a crunchy bite. So good!

I really think that moment in Mi Pueblo sums up my approach to food and cooking: Be curious, and always keep your eyes and heart open to new flavors, ingredients, and experiences. When I get home from a farmers' market or grocery store, I almost immediately dive into cookbooks and food media to learn more. I want to understand an ingredient's origin, its traditional uses, and how those traditional uses have been modified in modern cooking. I compare what I was told with what I thought I understood and what others are saying. Then I go to the kitchen and start experimenting. It's the best!

That spirit of exploration, my love of flavor, and my quest for culinary inclusiveness is at the heart of *Flavor+Us*. My aim here is to pass on my knowledge to you—all nineteen years of it!—and forge all my geeky food studies and experiences into an easy-to-navigate, delicious-to-eat-from, socially-conscious cookbook.

Toni Morrison once said, "If there's a book that you want to read, but it hasn't been written yet, then you must write it." *Flavor+Us* is born from Toni Morrison's mandate and my desire for a book that celebrates sustainable veggies, seafood, and meats, with a global palate.

If there's one place that reflects the values of my book, it's the corner of Ninth and Washington Streets in Oakland, where the Old Oakland Farmers' Market sits across from Swan's Market. The intersection is a few blocks from my old school, and I'd make pilgrimages there every Friday to spend my allowance on the year-round citrus and steaming chile y cheese tamales at the farmers' market. Tamale in hand, I'd cross Washington Street to watch Swan's fishmongers shuck fresh oysters, and florists present exciting, dramatic arrangements

to supersatisfied customers. The two venues hummed with community—in the shared seating, in the dozens of languages being spoken, in the mix of spices flowing past my nose. That corner is everything I—and the friends I've made through cooking—want from a cookbook.

The recipes in this book include ingredients and techniques from all over the world. I've worked in fine-dining restaurants and believe that the skills I learned there can be useful in *everyone's* kitchen. When I say "fine dining" or "fine foods," I really mean "high quality," which to me must include fair trade and equitable labor practices. Systemic racism breeds mediocrity, so it is impossible for a restaurant to be the best of the best with a kitchen that is all male or all one ethnicity. When I visited the kitchen of Le Bernardin, one of the country's most revered fine-dining establishments, under the leadership of Chef Eric Ripert, I was struck and encouraged by the diversity of the different teams and by how eager everyone was to share their techniques and methods with me. So, one of my goals with this book is to emphasize culinary techniques from many different cultures. For example, infusing an oil with herbs and citrus (see page 203) is a simple technique that can lead you in a million different directions. Pair it with Shorba Adas (Red Lentil Soup, page 99) or with Jalapeño Shrimp with Chard and Grits (page 129). Panfrying a cornmeal-dredged fish (see page 133) is a classic technique in Black American cooking. The dish works so well with Caribbean-influenced Curry Cabbage Steaks with Thyme and Red Pepper Butter (page 88) or the Quick Green Zesty Salad (page 79).

Yes, I've been on TV and *staged* (that's French cooking lingo for interned) in Michelin-starred restaurants, but I got my start in my mom's kitchen. I learned to cook with my mother, who is many things, but most relevant to this book, she is a traditional medicine herbalist and the center of our kitchen. She not only knows how to roast chiles until the exact moment before they turn bitter, she also sees the natural, edible world as a source of healing. With that comes an amazing sense of taste and a global mindset. When I was young, she took us to traditional Chinese medicine herbal shops, where I would look at everything around me and wonder how it all tasted and what it was used for. I got the message early that if it is part of the natural world, there is likely some use for it in eating, healing, or cooking.

Most of my mom's cooking tools were glass, wood, or metal. If my sisters and I were reheating anything, it was typically on the stove top or in the oven. To this day, Mom never uses a microwave, food processor, or kitchen gadgets. (I think that was one of the things that excited me most—and still excites me—about going on food competition shows and working in professional kitchens: the gadgets and professional tools.) I mention all of this because I don't want you to feel intimidated when I talk about technique. Having spent many eight-hour shifts peeling and prepping onions and breaking down tomatoes, I can tell you that lots of "technique" is just muscle memory! But it comes in handy in those moments when you *want* to make something but don't know where to start. If you're feeling uninspired, sometimes thinking about *how* you want to prepare something (roasted, panfried, raw) will be easier than figuring out *what* to cook.

But my goal with this book isn't just to help you learn to cook; I also want to help you expand your palate. Those sound like two different things, but they often go hand in hand. Whether you have a family like mine or not, you own your curiosity. In order to explore unfamiliar (and exciting!) ingredients—from chiles to chard to unusual cuts of meat and fish to unsung grains (like fonio, a gluten-free protein-packed wonder from Africa)—all you need is to find new stores to shop in, new grocery aisles to explore (online or in-person), and new recipes with your favorite ingredients.

Do you have a wide and curious palate? Here are a few questions that will help you find out:

QUESTION 1
Do you always want to try something new at a restaurant?

QUESTION 2
Do you shop at stores that cater to clientele from numerous food cultures and regions?

QUESTION 3
Have you ever seen an unfamiliar food on social media and wished to try it?

QUESTION 4
Do you imagine substitute ingredients or extra spices for traditional recipes?

QUESTION 5
Do people gawk at your school or office lunches?

If you answered "no" to a lot of the above, don't worry. This is a safe space to admit eating the same five dishes over and over again! Maybe you find them familiar and satisfying. Trust me, I know what that's about. But I also know how fantastic I feel when I try something new and it blows my mind. So, think of this book as a companion that holds your hand while you travel the world, dish by dish.

Mom says that people who say they dislike a particular food really haven't had it cooked in a way that suits their palate or with great technique. I have come to agree. I see it time and time again in restaurant settings, where a diner will say, "I hate XYZ ingredient, but the way the chef makes it here is so delicious—now I love it!"

The first step in expanding your palate is identifying what you love. Let's say it's a savory breakfast that includes eggs and rice. Then, ask yourself: what *exactly* do you love about the dish? Is it the technique—frying, sautéing, steaming? Is it the flavor profile—the spices or toppings? Is the dish indigenous to a particular region that you are drawn to?

Let's get more specific. Let's say you love tacos. Many Americans do, for good reason. If you love tacos, you probably love corn, jalapeños, queso, tomatoes, oregano, and slow-braised meat. That means you'll probably also love other corn dishes that appear on Mexican menus (but often don't get ordered by taco-loving Americans!)—dishes like tetela, torta, tlacoyo, or huarache.

In order to help you make these connections, I've written recipe headnotes that reveal ALL, giving them the Rahanna-interrogation-treatment, so that you get a dish's origins stories, evolution, how it found its way into my cookbook, and how the techniques behind it can be replicated and adapted to create dozens of other hits from around the world. Expanding your palate means taking what you know you love and pushing its boundaries.

So, strap in for the ride around the world and my kitchen! Regardless of your level in the kitchen—beginner, intermediate, super experienced and craving new inspiration—this book is for you. *Flavor+Us* is a guidebook for all of us on a journey to become a better cook and person, whether you're eight, eighteen, twenty-eight, or eighty.

Market Tips: Where to Shop

When you are buying food to eat, it is important to question how veggies, herbs, and fruits were grown and how the livestock that will become meat was cared for. Sustainable ingredients not only improve the taste of food; they also benefit the earth, the quality of farmers' work environments, and your kitchen. Supporting small business owners and companies with fair trade practices is equally important. If we are sincere about building a better world, why not support local and women-owned businesses? Why not seek out farmers at the farmers' market and small grocery and co-op stores owned by Black people, rather than buying industrially farmed products at a big-box store? It is not our responsibility alone to change corporate grocery practices, but it will not happen on its own. So, when I go shopping, I try to find out who owns what and who is in positions of leadership within the companies I buy from. What I have found is that the best stores and businesses are often not simply a grocery store, but a defiant resistance to the racist and sexist status quo. For example, there is a San Francisco co-op that was started by LGBTQ+ workers called Rainbow Grocery. One of their goals is to provide affordable vegetarian products that have a minimal negative impact, both ecologically and socially. My tip is to research the farmers' market in your area and try to see if you can get the majority of your grocery list there. Community-owned stores are also a great place to shop and buy products made nearby. There are many books and online resources about how to become a more conscientious shopper, but one of my favorites is *Black Food Geographies: Race, Self-Reliance, and Food Access in Washington, D.C.* by Ashanté M. Reese, which, using Washington, DC, as a microcosm of what happens all over the US, speaks to racist grocery store practices and provides resources to change these practices. Eating and shopping sustainably is not always easy or even accessible. Fast-food restaurants exploit their workers and their consumers, but in some places they are among the only options for eating out. Huge grocery stores are designed to be almost too convenient to resist, even though they are built on similarly exploitative labor practices. I encourage people to do whatever they can to support community, and that includes making the choices needed to support themselves and their family!

How to Make a Grocery List

Once you've figured out where to shop, the next step is figuring out what to buy! My biggest tip if you're headed to the farmers' market, grocery, or specialty store is to always have a list. Freshly baked Pullman loaf bread and tantalizing samples at the farmers' market always test my focus. I was visiting NYC to help with a Black diaspora-themed dinner for the James Beard House. Amazing chefs, including Adrian Lipscombe, Thérèse Nelson, Monica O'Connell, and Enrika Williams, had flown from as far as Alaska and Texas to prepare wonderfully spiced and warm dishes. But a few key ingredients were still missing, so I went to the farmers' market with Chef Kayla Stewart in search of peppers and a few herbs. On our way there, it started pouring rain! Rain plus October in New York City is not the best combo for an outdoor market. Thankfully, we had a grocery list and chef's orders to find what was needed. Otherwise, it would have been impossible for us to wander around the farmers' market without getting drenched.

That day I learned a lesson I'll never forget: Always have a list. I think taking five minutes to organize my grocery list saves me at least fifteen minutes of wandering around the store.

STEP 1.
On your phone or a piece of paper, write out each store aisle or section: produce, baking needs, dairy, eggs, frozen, grains, beans, sauces/condiments, butcher, seafood, and miscellaneous.

STEP 2.
Make a separate list of everything you need.

STEP 3.
Write each item in your list under its respective aisle, and you're done!

Pantry Staples

Here are a few essential ingredients I always have on hand.

COOKING OILS

I like to keep a neutral cooking oil such as grapeseed in my pantry. I also always have olive oil, and I think it is wiser to invest in a smaller amount of high-quality olive oil rather than a large amount of a lower-quality version.

SWEETENERS

I did not grow up in a home that had white sugar. Instead, we had the all-natural sugar that is found in many markets carrying goods from Caribbean and Spanish-speaking countries. We also always had maple syrup and dates. I love dates because they have a long pantry shelf life; even the oldest, most shriveled-up dried date still reconstitutes well with warm water in a blender. Local honey is a great way to support your regional artisans.

SALT

Salt seems pretty unassuming, but there is actually so much variety within the category. I tend to rely on a fine sea salt for cooking and coarse sea salt, like Maldon, for finishing. I also suggest having kosher salt for a last-minute brine or pickling project. Recently a local fisherman sold me a hand-harvested sea salt from Mexico that was so lovely. So, I recommend supporting ancestral traditions and seeking out the artisan salts in your community.

NUTS

I always have raw almonds, cashews, and other unsalted nuts in the pantry in case I want to make a quick nut milk.

RICE AND GRAINS

A selection of rice varieties is useful to have when you've gone to the farmers' market or gotten a load of veggies from a CSA box and you want to make a quick meal of veggies with a side of rice. Long-grain white rice and sushi rice are ones that I usually have in the pantry. Brown rice is delicious and nuttier, although it takes a bit longer to cook. I like to keep grains such as amaranth and quinoa in the pantry for last-minute hardy side dishes.

Essential Kitchen Tools

Invest in a good collection of cooking tools. Duplicates are great when there is more than one cook in the kitchen. I love all types of kitchen gadgets, but I developed the recipes in this book with the idea that everyone should be able to cook them without requiring a bunch of hard-to-find ingredients and tools. When it comes to purchasing, I recommend checking places such as large cooking stores as well as the local grocery store and resale thrift store. I've made some great finds at thrift stores, in particular antique items that are no longer made—such as a vintage lemon juicer that works better than a handheld one! Just remember, window shopping isn't just for clothes or big purchases.

MIXING BOWLS

Mixing bowls are always good to have around and are pretty essential, whether you're mixing dough or tossing a salad. I like to purchase glass mixing bowls, as they let you see what hasn't been thoroughly mixed at the bottom and they absorb fewer odors and colorings than plastic. When purchasing, try to look for a set because storage is always easier with items that can nest together.

MEASURING TOOLS

Measuring tools are important to get the proper amounts for any recipe. For measuring cups, I like metal ones that stack, and I like to have two sets. I keep one set for dry ingredients and liquid ones for wet ingredients. It is important to have measuring spoons, too. Having the exact teaspoon measurement is super helpful, especially when baking.

CHEF'S KNIFE AND PARING KNIFE

If you are just starting a knife collection or want to revamp your old one, I recommend starting with a chef's knife and a paring knife. Chef's knives are great for cutting ingredients such as root vegetables, meat, and pastries. A paring knife is excellent for detailed work like scoring bread dough and trimming stems from fruit. If you're just starting out or you want to conserve your money, opt for a cheap paring knife and spend more money on the chef's knife. The size is a matter of preference, but I recommend an 8-inch one. The handle on a chef's knife is very important, so test out how secure your grip feels and when it is most level for you. Many knife stores offer an area to test out the knives. I really recommend hat you take the time and try out as many as possible. The two main types of knives are forged and stamped. Forged knives are sturdier and typically heavier. They are also easier to sharpen but often more expensive. While stamped knives are cheaper and lighter, they are easier to break. You can tell if a knife is forged because it will usually have a bolster, which is a lip between the knife and the handle. Some people prefer the bolster as they feel it prevents accidental cuts. German and other European knives are very common but I also like exploring Japanese, Chinese, and Damascus steel knives. Artisan knife makers like Middleton Made Knives and Suisin are great resources, too.

Any good knife maker will provide advice on how to sharpen the knives. It is best to follow their instructions, as each knife is different, and the maker is the best at knowing how to keep the knife in its best and sharpest state.

KITCHEN TOWELS

I always have plenty of kitchen towels on hand. A kitchen towel can be used in so many ways. In professional restaurants, I use specific towels for proofing bread, taking a hot pan out of the oven, or even cleaning off the counters. At home, I use different colors to differentiate towels used for counter cleanups, for wiping the edge of a plate clean before serving, and those that actually touch food (for example, proofing bread).

KITCHEN TWEEZERS

I usually use small kitchen tweezers to plate dishes at dinner service in restaurants, but that's not their only use. I like to use kitchen tweezers to remove bones from fish, hairs from whole chickens, and even to remove things from small jars. When deciding which to purchase, I usually have at least two types: smaller tweezers and ones with a longer handle. At home, I like to use long tweezers to get foods out of jars and to remove things that are in a hot pan when a spatula or cooking spoon just won't work. Have you ever tried fishing a pickle out of an almost empty jar? Tweezers are thin enough to capture it without completely tearing apart the pickle in the process.

CUTTING BOARD

Cutting boards are self-explanatory, but I have a great tip: get a damp paper or kitchen towel and place it underneath your cutting board. The paper towel will prevent the cutting board from dangerously sliding when using it. I only have wooden cutting boards in my home, and those do require upkeep every once in a while. For everyday use, wash the cutting board with a gentle soap and dry immediately. If you notice odors or stains, a tablespoon of baking soda and a squeeze of lemon juice will usually clean both up. I like wooden boards better than plastic or glass cutting boards. Glass can be hard on knives, and plastic can absorb odors and colorings. Plastic can also shed over time, and the small grooves can retain moisture.

COOKING AND SERVING UTENSILS

I like wooden spoons and spatulas for everyday cooking. I like tongs for cooking and recommend the type that will close when not in use. Another useful cooking utensil is a pair of extra-long metal chopsticks to help with stirring and flipping. Rubber spatulas are great to have on hand when baking. They can help clear the sides of bowls to make sure everything is incorporated and to get every drop out of the bowl to avoid waste and reduce cleanup. A fine-mesh sieve and spider strainer are always useful when making smooth soups and sauces, and I've found the best way to clean them is to immerse them in a soapy bin and turn them upside down to scrub. For serving, I like to have a couple of wide-mouth serving spoons, a serving fork, and a salad set on hand.

SAUTÉ PAN

Stainless-steel sauté pans are great for panfrying, searing, and dry frying. I like to have different-size sauté pans for different occasions. Small sauté pans (8 inches) can be used for eggs, while large sauté pans (12 inches) are good for family-style meals like pastas, cooked veggies, and braised meats. If you buy only one, a standard 8- to 10-inch sauté pan works great for just about anything.

SAUCEPAN

Saucepans are great for sauces, but they also have so many more uses. I use them for small batches of grits, making caramels, and steeping teas. A saucepan normally holds 1 to 4 quarts and this is the range I like to stay within while shopping for them.

CAST-IRON SKILLET

If I have access to only one type of pan, I will always opt for an 8-inch cast-iron skillet. It works great on the stove top and in the oven. To maintain my cast irons, I clean with a gentle dish soap, dry, and then wipe the insides with a little neutral oil. You can skip these steps by buying preseasoned cast irons. Or you can take the time to oil your own, which doesn't take that long and just requires a little attention to detail!

STOCKPOT

Stockpots are great for so many recipes. Always opt for one with a lid that has a handle that you can lift easily and won't fall from your grip. I find that an 8-quart stockpot will work great for almost everything.

BAKING SHEETS

Baking sheets have so many different uses. I love to roast vegetables straight on a baking sheet for a really yummy caramelized flavor. Baking sheets can be used to make a variety of desserts, from cookies to roll cakes to meringues. I prefer rimmed versions, which result in fewer spills and less oven mess. If you have the option, definitely get rimmed half-sheet and quarter-sheet sizes. The quarter-sheet pan is always useful for reheating or keeping smaller portions warm.

INSTANT-READ THERMOMETER

This is the most expensive cooking item in this book, and I do think of it as an investment. If you are a meat eater, it will save a lot of time and food waste to use the thermometer to check for doneness. (Cutting into meat to see if it is done can dry it out and make the final cook uneven.) If you ever want to work with chocolate, sugary things such as caramel, or jellies, the instant-read candy thermometer makes the work so much more efficient.

BRUNCH MENU
INSPIRATION

Jalapeño Shrimp with Chard + Grits
(page 129)
+
Fruit Plate with Rose Scented
Honey (page 30)
+
Spinach Biscuits (page 38)
+
Strawberry Chamomile Pear Aguas
(page 184)

Breakfast + Breads —— 1

Breakfast is the first thing you put in your body when you wake up, so it should not only nourish you but also set you up for a wonderful and successful day. Not all mornings are created equal, and most days, people don't have time to prep a four-part breakfast. So, in this chapter, I offer quicker recipes for busy mornings, such as creole breakfast potatoes and a fruit plate with rose honey as well as longer recipes, like spinach biscuits and salsa scones, for a relaxed weekend or day off. Many of these recipes, for example the Five-Spice Granola (page 29), Salmon Bagel Spread (page 35), and Corn Cakes (page 37), can be made ahead of time and enjoyed for several days.

I grew up with a mom who was always planning for or prepping a part of the next meal so she had less work at mealtime. Professional kitchens similarly prep parts of dishes early in the work shift. It could be as simple as soaking grits (which results in not only a quicker cook time but also a better-quality, creamier dish), or making a hibiscus syrup whose flavors will deepen over time. I can't say I do this for every meal, but I do like to prep part of breakfast before I go to bed, so I wake up the next day to a breakfast halfway or nearly done. For instance, in this chapter, the dough for the Spinach Biscuits (page 38) can be made and cut the night before, stored in the freezer, and baked (without thawing) in the morning. Prepping ahead makes mornings feel more enjoyable and less rushed, especially when I'm groggy.

This chapter also features recipes for some of my favorite breads, including taboon, focaccia, and cornbread. Growing up, the breads we ate at home were either made from scratch or purchased directly from local bakeries. I once did an internship at Tartine Bakery in San Francisco, known for their wonderful pastries, cakes, and tartines. During my time there, I learned how to measure if something was proofed correctly. Proofing is a technique used to make yeasted dough soft and fluffy. We cut open croissants to check their proofing level. If the holes in between the baked croissant were large and uneven, that meant that it was overproofed. If the holes inside the croissant were small and symmetrical, they were perfectly proofed. I use this tip when making all my bread recipes. It's great to get even bubbles in dough without creating large gaps of air in the loaf or piece of bread.

FIVE-SPICE GRANOLA

Oats were used by Egyptians in the Twelfth Dynasty and in China two thousand years before that. This recipe is inspired by five-spice powder, which itself was created to represent the Wuxing theory. Wuxing translates roughly to "five elements": wood, fire, earth, metal, and water. These five elements are represented by five tastes: sour, bitter, sweet, pungent, and salty. The key ingredients in this granola are sour from the goji berries; sweet from the oats, sugar, and maple syrup; bitter from the roasted sunflower seeds; salty from the teaspoon of salt; and, finally, pungent from the orange zest. This technique of including the five tastes creates a balanced flavor that is great for the morning.

SERVES 6 TO 8

4 cups old-fashioned rolled oats

1 cup hulled sunflower seeds

⅓ cup grapeseed or another neutral oil

1½ teaspoons five-spice powder

3 tablespoons natural cane sugar

3 tablespoons maple syrup

1 teaspoon kosher salt

1½ cups dried goji berries

1 tablespoon orange zest (about 1 orange)

Preheat the oven to 325°F. Line a rimmed baking sheet with parchment paper. Sprinkle the oats and sunflower seeds on the prepared baking sheet, then drizzle the oil, five-spice, sugar, maple syrup, and salt over the top. Mix thoroughly with a large wooden spoon, spread the mixture out evenly, and let it sit while the oven finishes preheating.

Meanwhile, in a saucepan, combine the goji berries with 3 cups of water and heat over medium heat until steaming. Drain the berries, spread them out onto a separate baking sheet or cutting board, and reserve for later. (They should dry slightly but do not need to be dried completely.)

Bake the oat-seed mixture for 35 to 40 minutes, stirring halfway through, until the oats start to turn golden brown. Let cool completely on the baking sheet, about 1 hour.

Once cool, transfer the oat-seed mixture into a large container. Add the goji berries and orange zest and stir to combine. Serve in a bowl with your favorite type of milk. Store any leftovers in an airtight container at room temperature for up to 3 days.

FRUIT PLATE WITH ROSE SCENTED HONEY

I feel like a fruit plate is mandatory for a special brunch, but this one is also suitable for an everyday breakfast. This recipe gets you energized for your day without feeling weighed down by a big breakfast, and it's a superquick fix if you make the rose honey ahead of time. I find this recipe is very forgiving whether you use ripe or underripe fruit, and feel free to use any type of pear. If you prefer a firm texture, I suggest an Asian pear, Bosc, or Seckel. Otherwise, Anjou is a good all-around choice. I usually love putting a squeeze of lemon juice on apples as a snack, and this recipe combines that with fragrant rose honey. You may be left with a little extra honey, which I recommend using as a sweetener in tea, oats, or drizzled on yogurt and granola. You can use whatever fruit is in season; I like to do a pineapple and blueberry variation. Dress it up in a nice bowl or arrange it on a cute serving platter.

SERVES 4

1 pear, cored and cut into ¼-inch-thick slices

½ a pineapple, cored and cut into ¼-inch-thick slices

8 ounces strawberries, hulled and cut into ¼-inch-thick slices

¾ cup (6 ounces) blueberries

Zest of 1 lemon

Squeeze of lemon juice

¼ cup honey

1 tablespoon rose water

In a mixing bowl, gently toss the pear, pineapple, strawberries, and blueberries with a squeeze of lemon juice. In a small bowl, combine the honey and rose water. Drizzle the fruit with the scented honey, sprinkle with the lemon zest, and serve.

STEAMED EGG CUSTARD

Steamed egg custard is a great dish to make for breakfast. I almost always make it with my five-year-old brother because it is easy enough that children can help. This dish is silky and smooth and uses minimal ingredients. Steaming produces a wonderful soft custard without curds. You'll need four 6-ounce ramekins for this recipe and if you don't have a steamer insert, I offer a substitute below. I find that for best results, it's always good to bring the water to a simmer and then lower the heat when you add in the ramekins.

SERVES 4

4 eggs

½ teaspoon fine sea salt

1 teaspoon light soy sauce

1 teaspoon toasted sesame oil

Thinly sliced green onion for garnish

In a large pot with a steamer insert, simmer 2 cups of water over high heat. Place the steamer in the pot, and make sure the water is not touching the bottom of the steamer. If you do not have a steamer, form a few sheets of aluminum foil into 1-inch thick nest-like shapes large enough to hold a ramekin and sit securely while being steamed. You want the foil to be just slightly above the water.

In a mixing bowl, crack the eggs and gently whisk until the yolks and whites are combined. Add the salt and 1½ cups of water to the eggs. Gently whisk the salt and water into the eggs. Using a fine-mesh sieve, strain ½ cup of the egg mixture into each of the four ramekins.

Tightly seal the ramekins with foil or plastic wrap. Adjust the heat to medium-low and place the ramekins in the steamer or on top of the foil. Cover the pot with a lid and steam for about 10 minutes, until the eggs are still jiggly but not runny. You may need to do this step in two batches so each ramekin can fit.

Carefully remove the ramekins with tongs or a kitchen towel. Uncover the custards and drizzle with the soy sauce, sesame oil, and green onion.

BREAKFAST POTATOES WITH CRISPY FRIED HERBS + GARLIC

I've always loved breakfast potatoes, and few things pair better with potatoes than crispy garlic and herbs. Yellow potatoes are great in this recipe because of their starch level: they get really crispy on the bottom while staying soft on the inside. If you have a mandoline, use it to make thin slices of garlic easily, but if you don't have one on hand, a knife will also work.

SERVES 4

3 tablespoons extra-virgin olive oil

2 garlic cloves, thinly sliced lengthwise

Leaves from 1 (4-inch) sprig rosemary

1½ pounds yellow or Russet potatoes, scrubbed, patted dry, and cut into ½-inch cubes

Coarse sea salt

1½ teaspoons creole seasoning (page 209)

Line a plate with a few paper towels. Place the olive oil in a sauté pan, then add the garlic in an even layer (depending on the size of your pan, you might need to cook the garlic in batches). Cook over medium heat for about 4 minutes, until the garlic looks lightly tanned but not all the way brown, taking care not to burn it. With a spatula or slotted spoon, remove the garlic and place it on the towel-lined plate. With the pan still on medium heat, place the picked rosemary leaves into the pan and let them get crispy—this should take only a few seconds. Transfer the rosemary to the plate with the garlic and reserve the leftover oil.

Preheat the oven to 425°F. Place the potatoes on a rimmed baking sheet. Pour the infused garlic-rosemary oil over the potatoes and mix with a wooden spoon, making sure the oil and potatoes are evenly combined. Sprinkle with salt and the creole seasoning, then spread the potatoes into an even layer. Roast for 10 minutes, then flip the potatoes and roast for 15 more minutes, or until the bottoms look browned and crisp. Let the potatoes slightly cool, then top with the crispy garlic and rosemary and serve.

SALMON BAGEL SPREAD

Ohlone is the name of the indigenous nations that originated along the California coast from San Francisco to Big Sur. Some of the Ohlone traditional meats are duck, salmon, and quail, and their cooking techniques include smoking meats in manzanita, oak, and bay laurel wood. Oakland's Lake Merritt is an ancient salmon spawning area, and sometimes when walking the lake, I think about how Ohlone people used to fish there. While salmon spawning is rare nowadays, I wanted to acknowledge the contributions of the Ohlone in this recipe. While I love to get smoked salmon that uses the Ohlone culinary techniques, it may be hard to find, and in that case, any kind of cold-smoked salmon will work. I like the textural differences between the moistness of smoked salmon and the creaminess of baked salmon. Many salmon spreads call for poaching the salmon, but gentle roasting imparts a heartier flavor.

SERVES 4 TO 6

8 ounces skin-on salmon fillet, preferably freshwater king or coho

4 ounces cold-smoked salmon, minced

¼ cup finely diced red onion

1 tablespoon salt-cured or brined capers, unrinsed

1 heaping tablespoon minced fresh dill

3 tablespoons mayonnaise

Bagels for serving

Take the raw salmon out of the fridge while you preheat the oven to 350°F. Line a baking sheet or an oven-safe dish with parchment paper or aluminum foil. Place the salmon skin-side down on the baking sheet and bake for 15 minutes, or until it is pale pink. Let cool slightly, then remove the skin and check for any bones by lightly brushing a finger over the fillet. If you feel any bones, use kitchen tweezers or small tongs to remove them. Allow the salmon to cool in the fridge for about 15 minutes.

In a medium bowl, combine the whole roasted salmon fillet (if it has broken into pieces that is totally fine), smoked salmon, onion, capers, dill, and mayonnaise. Using a spoon or fork, gently mix until the roasted salmon has broken into bite-size pieces. Serve with bagels. Store leftovers, sealed, in the fridge for up to 4 days.

CORN CAKES

Whether called corn cakes, sweet cornbread, johnnycakes, or Shawnee cakes, this dish is loved by so many people. Essentially, this recipe is cornbread cooked like pancakes. Unfortunately, like much of Black culinary heritage, cornbread is often relegated to one type of serving. But cornbread can be more than just a dinner or lunch side! Corn—and, by extension, cornmeal—have been used throughout the African diaspora. South Africa's mealie bread, Jamaica's fried cornmeal fritter Festivals, and this American johnnycake are just a few examples. It is exciting to witness a product created from a plant that originated in Mexico extend its reach far and wide. Corn cakes can be dressed up with syrup or fruit, just like pancakes made with all-purpose flour. Just be prepared for your kitchen to be enveloped by a warm cornbread smell. I love a steaming plate of corn cakes in the morning, drizzled with a bit of maple syrup.

MAKES 6 CORN CAKES

½ cup fine-ground yellow cornmeal

1 cup all-purpose flour

1½ teaspoons baking powder

Pinch of fine sea salt

¼ cup natural cane sugar

1 cup 2% milk or unsweetened almond milk

2 tablespoons vegetable oil, plus more for cooking the pancakes

1 egg, beaten, or 3 tablespoons vegan liquid egg replacement

Syrup for serving

In a medium bowl, whisk together the cornmeal, flour, baking powder, and salt. In a separate small bowl, whisk together the sugar, milk, 2 tablespoons of oil, and egg. Add the wet mixture to the dry and stir with a wooden spoon or rubber spatula until combined.

In a skillet (preferably cast-iron), pour in just enough oil to barely coat the bottom of the pan. Heat to medium and add ⅓ cup of batter to the pan for each pancake. Depending on the size of your pan, you should be able to fit two or three corn cakes at a time. Do not disturb the pancakes and cook for 3 to 4 minutes on each side, until golden brown. Serve with syrup and enjoy!

SPINACH BISCUITS

This is one of my favorite breakfast recipes, and it is super easy to adjust with your own variations. Instead of spinach, you could substitute chard with the ribs removed; herbs like chives, thyme, or parsley; or shredded cheese. I love biscuits for breakfast, and the addition of spinach gives a great color and hint of flavor. Most weekends, my family makes a big breakfast—that can mean anything from Jalapeño Shrimp with Chard + Grits (page 129) to hash and scrambled tofu. We like to have one baked item that we make ahead of time, so we can focus on any stove top cooking that has to happen at the last minute. One of my favorite weekend memories is waking up to the sound of cooking and great smells swirling through the air.

A lot of this biscuit recipe involves sitting around and waiting for the dough to freeze or bake, so it's perfect for when you have other things to stand over and cook. The only tricky part is a step that requires folding over the dough in stages. This technique, called lamination, creates flaky layers of butter, and is commonly used in scallion pancakes and pastries like croissants or Danishes. It's crucial to develop soft-on-the-inside and crispy-on-the-outside layers, perfect for holding sturdy toppings and creamy sauces.

MAKES 8 BISCUITS

2 cups all-purpose flour

1 teaspoon natural cane sugar

2 teaspoons baking powder

½ teaspoon kosher salt

½ cup (1 stick) unsalted butter, frozen, plus 2 tablespoons melted

⅔ cup whole milk

⅔ cup packed spinach leaves

In a large bowl, whisk together the flour, sugar, baking powder, and salt. Grate the frozen butter on the large holes of a box grater, add the grated butter to the dry ingredients, and gently whisk. Place the flour-butter mixture in the freezer, along with your milk in a separate container.

While those ingredients chill, place the spinach leaves on a cutting board and shape them into a mound. Take a chef's knife and gently rock the knife back and forth over the spinach to create small pieces. The spinach pieces don't have to be perfectly similar, but you'll want them to be no bigger than the size of a pea.

continued

Remove the ingredients from the freezer and add the spinach to the flour-butter mixture. Slowly pour in the milk while stirring with a wooden spoon. The dough won't come together completely yet; it will look sandy with some moist parts.

Flip the bowl with your dough over onto the cutting board and gently pack the dough into a rectangle about the size of two hands and 1½ inches thick. Using your hands, fold the dough over like a greeting card, then lightly press the dough into a rectangle the size of a comic book. Don't worry if the dough is still shaggy with bits of dry flour. Repeat this folding process two more times with your hands. Flatten the dough with a rolling pin, roll it out to be about the same size as two hands, and then fold it over again. Repeat two more times with the rolling pin. Wrap your dough in plastic wrap and place in the freezer for 30 minutes. (The dough can stay in the freezer longer; just be sure to rest it on the counter-top until it can be easily cut for the next step.)

Meanwhile, preheat the oven to 400°F and line a baking sheet with parchment paper. Take the dough out of the freezer, unwrap it, and place it on a work surface. Removing as little dough as possible, cut the edges so they're straight. (You can bake these scraps, too.) Then cut the dough in half by splitting it down the length of the shortest side. Cut each half into four equal-size biscuits to make eight total. If you wish to freeze them at this stage, wrap them in plastic wrap or place them in a freezer bag without too much overlap so they thaw more easily.

Place the biscuits on the prepared baking sheet, but flip them so the side that was touching the cutting board while you sliced them is now facing up. (Cutting the biscuit pushes the edges of the biscuits down, so by flipping them over, you ensure the edges bake upward instead.) Brush with the 2 tablespoons of melted butter, then bake for 25 to 30 minutes, until the tops look golden brown. These biscuits are best enjoyed hot.

ALL GREEN FOCACCIA

In the effort to create something delicious with an easily accessible flour, I developed this all green focaccia. The chopped spinach in the dough imparts just a bit of moisture without overtaking the recipe, and the gentle mouthfeel is irresistible to me. Most of these ingredients are typically available from the farmers' market, and I think with such a simple recipe, fine ingredients are really important. I know Spain is the largest producer of olive oil, but I feel our California olive oils are so delectable. The truth is, if I am in any specialty store, the two things I always look for are olive oil and vinegar. I like to serve this with a bit of olive oil, balsamic vinegar, and bits of shaved Parmigiano Reggiano. It can work great as a sandwich bread, too. It is yummy the next day as long as it is covered or stored in an airtight container. You can reheat it gently at 325°F for 5 minutes.

**MAKES
1 LOAF**

Dough

2 cups plus 2 tablespoons all-purpose flour

½ teaspoon natural cane sugar

1 teaspoon flaky sea salt

1 cup baby spinach, finely chopped

⅔ cup water

1¼ teaspoons active dry yeast

2 tablespoons olive oil

Infused Oil

1 sprig rosemary

¼ cup extra-virgin olive oil

1 garlic clove, chopped (about 1 teaspoon)

1 teaspoon flaky sea salt

To make the dough, in a large bowl, combine the flour, sugar, and salt. Place the spinach in a small saucepan and add ⅔ cup of water. Heat over medium until lukewarm, making sure the water doesn't boil. Once the water is lukewarm, strain the water into a small bowl, leaving the spinach in the pan. Add the yeast to the water and stir. Once the yeast looks foamy, about 2 minutes, slowly pour it over the dry mixture, then add the olive oil, followed by the spinach. Stir with a spoon or knead with your hands for about 3 minutes, until the dough is smooth and slightly sticky. Cover the dough with a kitchen towel or plastic wrap and let it rest in a warm place for 45 minutes, until the dough has nearly doubled in size.

continued

While the dough is resting, make the infused oil. Pick the leaves off of the rosemary, leaving some pieces in small clusters and discarding the stems. Place in a small bowl or cup with the olive oil, garlic, and salt. Stir to combine, then set to the side. Allow to infuse for at least 5 minutes, or until the focaccia is done.

Preheat the oven to 425°F. Fold the dough completely in half two times. Re-cover and let rest for a final 10 minutes. Oil an 8-inch cast-iron skillet. Transfer the dough to the skillet, then use your fingers to evenly stretch the dough so it touches the edges of the pan. Pour the infused oil over the top of the dough and make indents all over with your fingertips. Bake the focaccia for 20 minutes, or until golden brown on top. Let rest in the pan for 8 minutes before cutting.

SALSA SCONES

To answer your first question, no, this is not a scone spread with salsa! Rather, it's a scone inspired by the flavor of salsa—specifically, pico de gallo or salsa fresca. I first realized my obsession with savory scones when staging at Tartine Bakery in San Francisco. I spent my time sorting through baked croissants to find the perfect evenly browned ones, piping éclairs, and layering cakes. On my last day, the superfriendly team let me choose two pastries to take home. I knew I had to pick the soft and spicy veggie scone. It had little moist pockets of corn and peppers and such wonderful flavor throughout. A few months later, I came back to Tartine and was heartbroken to discover the veggie scone had been swapped out with another savory scone. So, I began my quest to find another veggie scone in the Bay Area and finally found a great one at one of my favorite places for coffee, Red Bay. But soon after, the veggie scone was replaced with a sweet version, and I couldn't find any more veggie scones in the Bay (I checked relentlessly). I decided to take matters into my own hands. In my planning of my own version, I thought about my favorite elements in a veggie scone: slight spice, roasted veggies, and fragrant aromatics. The first thing that came to mind was salsa molcajete roja, so those are the flavors I decided to go with. One note about the technique: I find scones are best when just barely mixed together and highly recommend not overmixing or overworking the dough.

MAKES 8 SCONES

¼ white onion

1 jalapeño, at least 3 inches long

2 small Roma tomatoes

3 garlic cloves, unpeeled

2¼ cups all-purpose flour

2 teaspoons baking powder

2 teaspoons natural cane sugar

2 teaspoons fine sea salt

¼ cup unsalted butter, at room temperature and cut into 1-inch pieces

⅓ cup 2% milk

1 egg

Preheat the oven to 425°F. Place the onion, jalapeño, tomatoes, and garlic cloves on a baking sheet and roast for about 15 minutes, until slightly blistered. Leave on the baking sheet or transfer to a plate and let cool slightly. Lower the oven temperature to 350°F.

Meanwhile, line a baking sheet with parchment paper and set it aside.

continued

In a medium bowl, whisk together the flour, baking powder, sugar, and salt. Add the butter, working it in with your fingers, until the butter chunks are about the size of a pea.

Once the vegetables are cool enough to handle, peel the garlic and finely chop. Finely chop the onion. Peel the tomatoes and slice in half lengthwise. Remove and discard the seeds, so you're left only with the smooth outer layer of the tomatoes. Finely chop the tomatoes. Slice the jalapeño in half lengthwise, remove the seeds and stem, and then finely chop.

Add all the vegetables to the flour mixture. Pour in the milk, then stir with a flexible spatula or wooden spoon. The dough should come together but still look shaggy, with some flour falling away. Flip the bowl of dough onto a cutting board and pat the dough into a 5-inch circle, pressing any loose flour into the dough. Cut the dough into 8 triangular pieces, like a pizza. Place on the prepared baking sheet.

In a small bowl, whisk together the egg and 2 tablespoons of water to make an egg wash. Using a pastry brush, lightly coat the tops of the scones with the egg wash. (You won't use all of the egg.) Bake for 45 minutes, or until the tops and bottoms look golden brown. Let the scones cool completely before serving.

CONCHA SCONES

I love the brilliance of Mexican desserts. In many ways, Mexican desserts are actually not super sweet. Historically, the sugar used is not a white granulated sugar but a sugar called piloncillo, which has brown-sugar-molasses richness. I have so many memories of my abuelita and us drinking cinnamon tea and eating pan dulce. The cream-filled horn (curerno) or the molasses-rich pig-shaped cookie (marranito) are iconic favorites, but for me, the concha is pure perfection. It is hardy enough to withstand a dunk into coffee con leche, Mexican cinnamon tea, or Mexican hot chocolate without crumbling or adding too much sweetness. A scone is similar to me in that it doesn't need to be too sweet (or even sweet at all). Here, the topping, which goes over the scone almost like a sprinkle of sugar, adds just enough sugar without overpowering the base. While typically scones are eaten with clotted cream or jelly, these scones are completely self-sufficient; they don't need anything but themselves to be delicious and satisfying.

MAKES 8 SCONES

Topping
½ cup all-purpose flour

¼ cup unsalted butter, at room temperature

⅓ cup natural cane sugar

5 drops red food coloring

Scones
2¼ cups all-purpose flour

½ cup natural cane sugar

½ teaspoon salt

1½ teaspoons baking powder

½ cup (1 stick) unsalted butter, at room temperature

1 egg lightly beaten

½ cup whole milk

To make the topping: In a small bowl, use a fork to combine the flour, butter, sugar, and red food coloring. Once the butter has been incorporated, use your hands to knead the topping dough into a smooth texture. You may want to wear gloves to prevent the food coloring from tinting your hands pink. The mixture should resemble a light pink sugar cookie dough. Set the mixture aside.

To make the scones: In a large bowl, whisk together the flour, sugar, salt, and baking powder. Once everything is combined, add in the butter. Using a fork, press and stir the butter until the dough forms little pea-sized balls. Add the egg and milk. With the fork or

continued

a rubber spatula, slightly stir together the ingredients just until the flour is almost incorporated. It should look sandy and dry on the outside. Empty the dough onto a cutting board. Fold the dough over onto itself until it looks evenly moist with small dots of butter. Gently press the dough into its original bowl, almost as if it's a mold. Set aside.

Preheat the oven to 350°F. Line a baking sheet with parchment paper or aluminum foil and set it aside. Roll the topping into a ball and place onto a piece of parchment paper, wax paper, or plastic wrap. Roll or press the topping out into a 5- to 6-inch circle.

Flip the bowl with your dough over onto a cutting board, and flatten into a 5- to 6-inch disc. Place the topping on top of the scone dough with the parchment paper facing up. Carefully remove the parchment paper from the topping and gently press the topping to seal it to the scone dough. This should look kind of like a frosted sugar cookie.

With a large chef's knife, cut the dough into 8 triangular pieces. To decorate the scones, you can get creative or stick to more traditional designs. I like to cross hatch the topping of the scones with a paring knife, or make the more traditional cut of five curved lines along the top meant to resemble a concha (or shell). The knife should score right before it reaches the actual scone dough. If you don't want to use a knife, you can make the curved lines with a metal measuring cup. Hold the cup facing downward and press one edge of the cup down into the topping to make five evenly spaced curved lines. Once all the scones have a design, arrange them at least 1½ inches apart on the prepared baking sheet. Chill in the fridge 10 minutes before baking. Bake for 20 minutes, or until the bottom edges start to look golden brown. Let cool for at least 10 minutes. Serve immediately or store in a sealed bag or container for up to 1 week.

TABOON BREAD

Taboon, like a lot of dishes that originate from cultures that predate the English language, gets its name from the technique and tool used to create this bread (the taboon is a clay oven that gives a gentle char). Taboon is often eaten with main meals like musakhan, shawarma, or small mezes because of its deliciousness and ability to hold sauces. Taboon and mezes are eaten all over the world and are common in different cultures. I grew up eating the Palestinian version of taboon. I really love how well it pairs with the hummus on page 67. This recipe is one of the quickest bread recipes I've made. The dough is naturally sticky, so do not feel like you missed a step or need to add more flour. Once the dough rises, it should become less sticky and more manageable. Plan to make this bread right before you want to eat it, as it's best enjoyed warm from the oven. To mimic the char of the taboon oven, place your cooked bread over an open flame on your stove for a few seconds. This will achieve a more toasted flavor and a nicely charred look as well.

SERVES 5

1 teaspoon active dry yeast

1 cup plus 2 tablespoons lukewarm water

2½ cups organic all-purpose flour

1 teaspoon fine sea salt

2 tablespoons extra-virgin olive oil

In a small bowl, combine the yeast and water. Stir and set to the side for 5 minutes so the yeast can activate and becomes frothy. In a large bowl, whisk together the flour and salt. Slowly add the yeast-water mixture and olive oil into the flour mixture and stir with a rubber spatula to combine. On a dry work surface, knead your dough into a loose ball. It will be sticky, so just dust some flour onto your hands and go with it. Lightly oil a separate large bowl, then transfer the dough ball into the oiled bowl. Let the dough rest, covered with a kitchen towel, for 20 minutes.

After 20 minutes, the dough will have risen slightly but not look too different. Split the dough into five equal pieces and roll into rounds. Flour a large cutting board and, with your palm, spread each piece of dough into a 4- to 5-inch disc. Once shaped, let the dough rest on the cutting board, covered loosely with a kitchen

continued

towel, for 5 minutes. Place a baking sheet or cast-iron skillet on the middle rack of the oven and preheat to 350°F.

Place up to three circles of dough onto the baking sheet or two circles in your cast-iron skillet; they may touch but shouldn't overlap. They might stretch into ovals when you transfer them, which is okay, but try to keep them no more than 5 inches long to maintain the right thickness. Bake for 8 minutes. The dough should look pale but firm. Flip with a pair of tongs, then bake for 8 more minutes. The bread should have golden brown spots when it's done. Bake the remaining dough discs. For a nice char, toast your bread on an open flame on your stove top for about a minute per side. Wrap the bread in a kitchen towel, let cool slightly, and serve while still warm.

COCKTAIL PARTY
MENU INSPIRATION

Charbroiled Oysters (page 72)
+
Classic Hummus (page 67)
+
Taboon Bread (page 51)
+
Ginger Spritzer (page 179)
+
Sharab Rose Raspberry Shrub
(page 183)

Snacks —— 2

These recipes are my go-tos when I'm having friends over for a movie night, hosting a dinner party and need snacks available before the main courses are served, or I'm just looking for something to nibble on by myself. These bites remind me of my time interning at restaurants, when I would try little nibbles of food that were not fit to be served due to a little inconsistency or mess-up. When working all day in a hot kitchen, a nice warm bite of incredible food is always a pick-me-up. So I think of the recipes in this chapter as small pockets of joy. Feel free to mix and match the recipes from this chapter with recipes from other chapters to make a full meal. For example, I really like spreading hummus on Taboon Bread (page 52) and adding grilled veggies to make a quick sandwich.

GARLIC PANFRIED PLANTAINS

This is one of my favorite recipes for cooking demonstrations because it's quick, satisfying, and has great flavor. I originally created it when I was invited to be a food contest judge at the Gilroy Garlic Festival, a beloved Northern California food festival that celebrates all things garlic, including savory and sweet items, like garlic fries and garlic ice cream. These fried plantains are an ideal snack for garlic lovers and those who like sweet and salty flavors, but they can also be served as a side dish at lunch or dinner. On Fridays, my mom, two sisters, and I would often go to the farmers' market and then stop nearby at Specialty Foods, a shop owned by Nina Cruz, that carried Caribbean and African food and beauty products. It was the Bay Area's oldest African and Caribbean store until it closed in 2019. The shelves were always packed with spices and marinades that could make your mouth water by just looking at them. Most important, there was a shelf of plantains in different stages of ripeness. Some people feel there is no such thing as an overripe plantain; they are sweeter and softer when the yellow peel has turned completely black. The riper the better for this recipe.

SERVES 2 TO 4

1 tablespoon neutral oil, such as avocado or grapeseed

3 garlic cloves, finely minced

1 tablespoon unsalted butter

2 ripe plantains, peeled and cut diagonally into 1½-inch-thick slices

¼ teaspoon kosher salt

1 tablespoon flat leaf parsley leaves, chopped

Heat a large skillet over medium heat, then add the oil and garlic. Cook until the garlic is lightly browned, about 3 minutes, then remove the garlic and set it aside. There will be a bit of oil left in the pan.

In the same pan, melt the butter over medium-low heat. Working in batches so as not to crowd the pan, fry the plantains for 3 to 5 minutes on each side, until soft and lightly browned. Transfer to a small serving plate and sprinkle with ⅛ teaspoon of the salt. Repeat with the remaining plantains, then sprinkle with the crispy garlic and the parsley and serve.

SWEET + SALTY NORI POPCORN

I loved seaweed growing up. We often had nori on hand for sushi nights: we would prep a variety of fillings and then my sisters and I would roll our own sushi to our hearts' content. But my favorite form of seaweed by far was the small containers of nori sheets, which come in flavors like sea salt, teriyaki, or olive oil. For me, it was always about the underlying sweet flavor in seaweed. This recipe calls for natural cane sugar, which has a variety of marketing names. So, if you can find an all-natural cane sugar, I really think the less-processed taste is worth it. Making popcorn on the stove gives the kernels a slightly toasty flavor. I like to put the popcorn into a cake pan after it's done. This makes the popcorn turn into clusters and works really great if you're sharing with others.

MAKES 5 CUPS

1 (4- to 5-gram) pack roasted nori seaweed snacks

2 tablespoons neutral oil, such as avocado or grapeseed

⅓ cup popcorn kernels

3 tablespoons natural cane sugar

Lightly oil an 8-inch round cake pan.

In a blender, pulse the seaweed until you get small flakes. Place the seaweed in a small bowl and set it to the side.

Set a stockpot with a lid on high heat. Add the oil and 2 kernels of popcorn and cover with the lid. Wait until both kernels pop, and then remove them from the pot with a slotted spoon.

Off the heat, add the rest of the kernels. Quickly stir, then cover and place back on the heat. Cook for 3 to 4 minutes, until the popping stops, occasionally shaking the pot to loosen unpopped kernels. Remove the pot from the heat, stir in the seaweed flakes and sugar, and pour the popcorn into the cake pan. Weight the popcorn with a dinner plate to form it into the pan.

Let the popcorn cool for 5 minutes, then turn it upside down onto a serving plate or small cutting board to unmold the popcorn. To serve, roughly cut the popcorn disc into four pieces. The popcorn will crumble, but some pieces will stay in clusters. Store any leftovers in a sealed container for up to 2 days.

SPICED TORTILLA CHIPS

Hot tortilla chips are my all-time favorite, and these chips taste great right after they're fried. The chile California gives a rich, toasty flavor with a subtle spiced kick. Can't find powdered chile California? It might be listed as New Mexican chile, or you can use smoked paprika. If your tortillas are on the thicker side or freshly made, I recommend frying the tortillas for an additional minute.

MAKES 20 CHIPS

½ cup neutral oil, such as avocado or grapeseed, plus more as needed

5 corn tortillas, each cut into 4 even strips

¼ teaspoon kosher salt

¼ teaspoon powdered chile California or smoked paprika

Line a large bowl with paper towels.

Pour the oil into a small saucepan, adding more if needed to cover the entire bottom of the pan. Set the pan over high and heat the oil until it reaches 345°F on an instant-read thermometer. (If you don't have a thermometer, drop a small piece of tortilla into the oil. The oil should bubble around the tortilla.)

When the oil is hot, lower the heat to medium. Fry the tortilla strips in batches, starting with the largest pieces and making sure that the strips don't overlap, for 2 minutes, or until the corners start to curve up and the bottoms get crispy. With chopsticks or tongs, gently turn over the chips. Fry for 1 more minute and then transfer the chips to the paper towel—lined bowl. Repeat with the remaining tortilla strips.

Once all the tortillas are fried, sprinkle the salt and chile over the chips, and shake the bowl to distribute the seasonings. (There's no need to remove the paper towels.) Enjoy the chips with your favorite dip or Salsa Molcajete Roja (pages 64–65)!

SALSA MOLCAJETE ROJA

This salsa is my go-to for chips, tacos, quesadillas, and really anything else. It lasts a superlong time, and I like to make it every other week, so I always have some in the fridge. You may have heard that jalapeños vary wildly in their spice levels. This is because when the jalapeño plant lacks water and is stressed, it produces a spicier pepper. For this recipe, you can leave the seeds in for a spicier salsa, or remove them. If I'm using this as a dip for chips, I like to leave the seeds in. But if I'm going to pour it over tacos or tamales, I tend to leave out the seeds for a balanced taste, or I reserve the seeds and add them at the end once I see how spicy the salsa turns out. If you think the ingredients are getting too dark when you're roasting them, don't worry. This char adds the best depth of flavor to the salsa, and you want the ingredients to be well charred so each ingredient is soft enough to crush in your molcajete. The Mexican version of a mortar and pestle, molcajete y tejolote have been used for the last twenty centuries and are usually made of basalt (a volcanic rock). If you don't have a molcajete or a mortar and pestle, a bowl is a good substitute: use a cup or jar to grind the ingredients. You could also use a blender.

MAKES 1½ CUPS

1 pound Roma tomatoes

2 garlic cloves, unpeeled

⅛ onion

1 jalapeño

Fine sea salt

½ bunch cilantro leaves, coarsely chopped

Preheat the oven to 425°F. Line a baking sheet with aluminum foil. Place the tomatoes, garlic, onion, and jalapeño on the baking sheet. Roast for 15 minutes, or until both sides are charred-looking. Remove the garlic from the pan and set it aside. Turn over the tomatoes and jalapeño, then roast for another 15 minutes. By the end, the tomatoes and jalapeño should be soft and blistered with blackish-brown spots. Let the ingredients cool for about 5 minutes, until comfortable to touch. Peel the garlic and use the smaller end of the tejolote or pestle to crush the garlic inside the molcajete (or mortar). Do the same with the onion. With a knife, remove the stem from the charred jalapeño. Now you can choose your own spice level: you can either remove the seeds for more garlic and tomato flavor (reserve them so you can adjust the heat level later), or leave the seeds in and enjoy a pretty spicy salsa.

Using the wider end of your tejolote, gently press the jalapeño into the molcajete along with 1 teaspoon of salt until the jalapeño is mashed into smaller, less-than-bite-size pieces. Add the tomatoes in batches, by gently pressing with the tejolote until the tomatoes combine with the jalapeño. Try to work the chunks of tomatoes out along the sides of your molcajete to incorporate everything. If your molcajete gets too full, use a large spoon to transfer some liquid to a separate bowl and add it back in later. (I use the spoon to stir the salsa inside the molcajete if the tomatoes seem particularly juicy.)

Fold in the cilantro and transfer to a serving bowl. Taste for salt and add a pinch if needed. Enjoy immediately, or store in a sealed container in the fridge for up to 2 weeks.

Variation: Using a Blender

Roast the vegetables as instructed, then pulse the garlic, jalapeño, tomatoes, and 1 teaspoon of salt, all together, for about 3 seconds, until chunky. Stir in the cilantro, taste for salt, and serve.

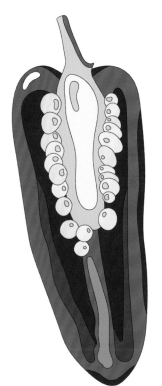

QUICK GUACAMOLE

Guacamole usually is avocado mashed with chopped tomatoes, onion, salt, lime, and cilantro. I found that you can make guacamole in under five minutes by carefully folding in a salsa roja. I really like to eat this recipe with the Spiced Tortilla Chips (page 63). If you want to add an extra layer of flavor, you can add in chopped cilantro when the salsa goes in.

SERVES 4

2 ripe avocados

¼ cup Salsa Molcajete Roja (page 64) or another chunky salsa roja

½ teaspoon coarse sea salt

1 lime wedge

Cut the avocados in half, remove the pits, and scoop the green flesh into a small bowl. With a fork, mash the avocados until almost smooth but slightly chunky. Guacamole is very forgiving, and if your avocados aren't the ripest, you can still achieve a smooth texture with the fork mashing. Gently fold in the salsa, sea salt, and a squeeze of lime. Eat immediately, or store in an airtight container for a couple of days. If the top layer appears brown, just scoop the top layer off and discard.

CLASSIC HUMMUS

This garbanzo-based hummus takes less than thirty minutes, so if you have extra time, I recommend making Taboon Bread (page 52) to go along with it. Hummus is also a great snack with cut raw veggies and different types of chips. You can even serve hummus alongside your dinner. But my family's most common use is in sandwiches on almost any kind of bread, with roasted veggies (like zucchini or red bell pepper) and topped with sprouts.

SERVES 4

1 (14-ounce) can garbanzo beans, rinsed and drained

¾ teaspoon fine sea salt

¼ cup tahini, well stirred

4 teaspoons lemon juice

2 garlic cloves

¼ cup extra-virgin olive oil, plus more for drizzling

1 jalapeño, diced and seeded

Sprinkle of sumac, smoked paprika, or cayenne

In a blender, combine the beans, salt, tahini, lemon juice, and 2 tablespoons of water. Using a grater, grate the garlic cloves directly into the blender. When the garlic gets to a marble size, just save for stock or basting as to not accidentally grate your fingers. Blend, starting at the lowest setting and gradually increasing to the highest. Garbanzo beans can be dense and the slower movement allows for the beans to break down easier. Gradually add the ¼ cup of oil while blending. If the hummus gets stuck in the blender, turn it off and use a spatula to loosen anything stuck around the blade. Process the hummus until smooth and creamy.

To serve, place the hummus in a bowl and make a divot in the center by dragging a teaspoon in a circular shape. Drizzle with olive oil to fill the divot. Finish by sprinkling with the diced jalapeño and sumac along the edge.

RAINBOW VEGGIE CRACKERS WITH AVOCADO HERB DIP

If you are someone who loves a creamy guacamole or creamy dip of any manner, this will likely be your new go-to dip! This dip pairs so well with the Rainbow Veggie Crackers shown in this recipe, but it also goes well with grilled veggies, Spiced Tortilla Chips (page 63), and the iconic humble potato chip (whether thin, ridged, or kettle). For cooked foods, I've use this as a dip for veggie fritters, slow-cooked salmon, roasted chicken, and tofu. Just like how the ascorbic acid from a lime or lemon in guacamole prevents it from browning too quickly, the ascorbic acid from the fresh dill, mint, and capers in this recipe allows the dip to sit in the fridge for a day ahead of time. Beyond two or three days, the dip will still be tasty, but it will have a brown tint.

SERVES 4

Cracker Dough

5 tablespoons unsalted butter, at room temperature

¼ teaspoon fine sea salt

1 cup all-purpose flour, plus extra for dusting

¼ cup water

1 tablespoon store-bought pesto

2 teaspoons carrot juice

2 teaspoons beet juice

Sprinkle of flaky sea salt

Avocado Herb Dip

1 avocado

5 ounces Greek yogurt

1 packed tablespoon mint leaves

1 packed tablespoon picked dill

2 tablespoons drained capers

1 teaspoon fine sea salt

To make the dough: In a medium mixing bowl, add the butter, salt, and flour. With a fork in one hand and knife in the other, cut the butter into pea-sized balls. Drizzle in the water bit by bit and gently mix until it forms a smooth dough. Dust a cutting board with flower, pour out the dough, and divvy it into 3 equal pieces. Now we can color them! In a small bowl, place 1 piece of dough and pour the pesto over it. Knead with your hands until well combined. If needed, you can dust your hands with flour to combine it quicker. Once mixed, remove the pesto-infused dough from the bowl, rinse the bowl, and repeat the process for the

continued

remaining two doughs with the carrot juice and the beet juice. For the beet juice, I recommend wearing gloves while kneading the dough as the beet juice can temporarily stain skin.

Preheat the oven to 350°F. Line a baking sheet with parchment paper and set it aside.

On a floured work surface, roll out the pesto dough until it has the thickness of a nickel. Trim the edges of the dough to get a nice rectangular shape and cut the dough into one-inch-sized squares. Place the pesto squares onto the parchment paper in a single layer. Repeat the same steps with both the carrot dough and the beet dough. If you'd like, you can reroll out the trimmings of each dough. Top each cracker with a small sprinkle of flaky sea salt. Bake the crackers in the oven for 10 to 14 minutes or until a few of the crackers are just browned on the edges. Place them into a container and let them cool.

Meanwhile, make the avocado herb dip: In a blender, combine the avocado, yogurt, mint, dill, capers, and salt and blend for just a few seconds. You still want to see the herbs and capers in the dip. Once blended, place into a bowl and enjoy with the rainbow crackers. Store leftover crackers in an airtight container for up to 1 week.

Variation: Using a Blender to Make the Veggie Juice

The recipe uses pesto and veggie juices for flavoring. If you don't have the veggie juices, you can make the juice with a blender or grater and a strainer. For example, the carrot juice can be made by blending half a carrot with three tablespoons of water and straining the liquid. If you don't have a blender, try grating half a carrot, adding three tablespoons of water, and then pressing the mixture into a sieve to strain out the juice. Spinach is a another veggie that has a lot of natural liquid. Finely chop a handful and add two or three tablespoons of water. After 15 minutes, you should have enough bright green liquid to use.

Variation: Different Cracker Flavors

For the three cracker choices, you could switch things up and try these options in place of the pesto, carrot juice, and beet juice.

- tablespoon of tomato sauce
- teaspoon of grated cheese, such as Parmigiano or Reggiano cheese
- tablespoon of dried or finely chopped fresh oregano
- tablespoon of enchilada sauce
- teaspoon of crumbled Cotija cheese and teaspoon of finely chopped cilantro

CHARBROILED OYSTERS

Charbroiled oysters always make me think of my time in Louisiana, when Chef Emeril Lagasse invited me to intern in his restaurants Emeril's and Meril. I even got to help out with a royal tricentennial luncheon for the king and queen of Spain, where Chef Nina Compton made an amazing salad with sunflower petals. I worked a lot during this internship, because I spent a week at Chef Emeril's restaurants and then went to intern at Chef Compton's Compère Lapin afterward. One of my favorite stations to work was the oyster bar at Compère Lapin. I would shuck oysters side by side with other cooks and talk about all things food. I love oysters, especially Kumamoto oysters, but please feel welcome to substitute your favorite for this dish. That said, I believe this recipe works best with a smaller oyster. An oyster knife will make your work a lot easier here.

MAKES 12 OYSTERS

4 garlic cloves, minced

2 tablespoons unsalted butter

¼ cup shredded Parmesan

2 tablespoons chopped fresh parsley

12 Kumamoto oysters, freshly cleaned and shucked (see Cook's Note, opposite)

Warm a saucepan over medium heat, then add the garlic and the butter. Cook on medium heat for 4 minutes, until the garlic is golden. Transfer the garlic butter to a medium bowl and mix in the Parmesan and parsley.

Preheat the broiler with an oven rack raised closest to the broiler. Place the oysters on a baking sheet. To keep them from falling over, you can balance them, leaning them against the cleaned top shells, or you can scrunch rings of aluminum foil around the shells to make little seats for the oysters. Divide the garlic butter mixture among the oysters by topping each with about 1 heaping teaspoon. Use care to scoop up garlic in each teaspoon. Broil for 2 to 3 minutes, until the Parmesan is melted and lightly browned. Let the oysters cool slightly before enjoying.

COOK'S NOTE: HOW TO CLEAN AND SHUCK OYSTERS

You'll need an oyster knife, a kitchen towel, a cutting board, and a shellfish brush or any hard bristle cleaning brush.

1. If the oysters come in a netted bag, leave the oysters in the bag (if the oysters are not in a bag, use a bowl that will keep the oysters snug together without the chance of overflowing with water), and put the oysters in a large bowl with 1 cup of ice and enough cold water to cover the shells. Soak the oysters for 30 minutes to help release some grit.

2. Meanwhile, add ice to a wide bowl or other serving vessel with a lip. The goal is for the cleaned oysters to rest on top of the ice without sitting in melted ice water.

3. With a shellfish brush (or any food brush with natural stiff bristles), scrub each oyster and rinse under cool water. It's important to get the shells as clean as possible since you'll slurp the oyster meat out of them.

4. It's time to shuck: Take one oyster and position it on a cutting board so the long side is facing you and the rounded shell is on the bottom. Wrap half of it in a clean kitchen towel, so one of the shorter sides is peeking out. (Among these short sides, the thicker side is called the hinge, and the thinner side has the adductor muscle that attaches the oyster to the shell. You can open the oyster from either side, but I think the thinner side is easier.) Lodge your oyster knife into a crevice between the two shells. Twist and pry your knife down until the shell pops open.

5. Wipe off your blade on the towel and cut along the top of the oyster, separating the top shell from the bottom. Set aside the top shell. Use your knife to cut under the oyster meat, releasing it from the bottom shell so it's easier to slurp later. Check for and discard any shell fragments, then place the shucked oyster in its bottom shell on the bed of ice. Repeat with the rest of your oysters.

QUICK GO-TO LUNCH
MENU INSPIRATION

Respect Ancient Goddesses Salad
(page 80)
+
Spiced Tortilla Chips (page 63)
+
Oat Horchata (page 193)

Salads, Sides + Soups —— 3

I normally get up early, and by the afternoon, I want something that will fill me up but still save space for dinner. This chapter's recipes solve just this problem. Many of the recipes here can be combined to make a great meal. I love pairing the Shorba Adas (Red Lentil Soup; page 99) with the Respect Ancient Goddesses Salad (page 80). The herby oil that's drizzled on top of the soup is enhanced by the fresh herbs in the salad. Dishes like the lentil soup, Creamy Refried Beans (page 96), and Arroz Rojo (page 97) can be sealed and refrigerated or even frozen for later, and the Respect Ancient Goddesses Salad yields extra dressing (or veggie dip) to store for later or even use for marinades. I suggest this salad hands-down if you want to plan ahead for the week. But if you are in a rush or just want to use one bowl, I suggest the Quick Green Zesty Salad (page 79). Each ingredient is layered into the salad bowl to create no leftover dressing and is an easy one-bowl assembly and cleanup. Sides, soups, and salads are a wonderful addition to any meal, or they can be teamed up with one another to create an amazing spread.

QUICK GREEN ZESTY SALAD

I am often in a rush to complete work and get to tennis practice in the afternoons. I created this salad to be a satisfying and quick lunch. Instead of turning the dressing ingredients into an emulsion, I opted to pour each ingredient right on top of the salad, which resulted in it tasting even more flavorful than usual. Having each ingredient on its own instead of coated in oil makes the taste cling to the leaves, rather than getting stuck at the bottom of the bowl. I recommend grating the lemon for the zest first, then squeezing the juice to make it a bit easier.

SERVES 4

1 head romaine lettuce, bottom 1 inch removed, leaves separated and cut into 1-inch strips

2 garlic cloves

1 tablespoon grated lemon zest

3 tablespoons lemon juice

2 tablespoons agave nectar

3 tablespoons extra-virgin olive oil

½ teaspoon kosher salt

Freshly ground black pepper

Place the romaine in a large salad bowl. Using a Microplane grater, grate the garlic over the lettuce, stopping once the cloves are the size of a marble so you don't accidentally grate your finger. (Save these garlic bits for another purpose, such as making stock or spoon-basting foods with an infused oil.) Sprinkle the lemon zest onto the lettuce and toss. Add the lemon juice and agave, then toss again. Drizzle the oil over everything, then finish by sprinkling with the salt and some pepper. Toss and serve immediately.

RESPECT ANCIENT GODDESSES SALAD

This salad dressing is influenced by Green Goddess dressing, which was created at the Palace Hotel in San Francisco. The story goes that the salad was created to celebrate a white actor who played a character named Raja of Rukh in a play set "in a remote area of the Himalayas" titled The Green Goddess. It was subsequently made into a movie with a brownface ensemble that used fake, racist Indian accents and wore afros. Every time I hear the Green Goddess name, I cringe, thinking of the racist associations.

When I was naming this dish, I remembered the first time I saw the Green Tara image in the Asian Arts Museum in SF. My mom told me that Green Tara is known as the mother of all Buddhas and is both compassion and action together. So, when we think of Green Goddess, I hope we will begin to look beyond our recent racist experiences and delve deep into the ancient past to find a more nuanced understanding. I wanted to use this recipe as an expression of defiance for things with racist origins that have become commonplace.

SERVES 4

Salad Dressing

Leaves from ½ bunch flat-leaf parsley

¼ cup plain Greek yogurt or nondairy plain yogurt

1 avocado (about ½ cup)

¼ cup lightly packed coarsely chopped chives

¼ cup lightly packed fresh dill leaves

½ cup apple juice

1 teaspoon fine sea salt

1 head romaine lettuce

Your favorite croutons and other salad toppings (such as chopped raw veggies: red onion, tomato, cauliflower, or broccoli) for serving (optional)

To make the salad dressing: In a blender, combine the parsley, yogurt, avocado, chives, dill leaves, apple juice, and sea salt. Blend until the mixture looks light green with small specks of dark green leaves and stems.

Place the romaine on a cutting board and, starting from the tip, cut it into 1-inch strips until you reach the end of the bunch where it is mostly white stem. Discard the stem. Toss the romaine in a big bowl with ¼ cup of the salad dressing, then gradually add more dressing if desired. Top with your favorite croutons and toppings, if desired. Store leftover dressing in an airtight container in the fridge for 2 to 4 days.

BRAISED COLLARDS WITH PICKLED STEMS

My family has so many recipes for leafy green veggies. It seems many people have a variety of greens recipes and methods. The variations include adding tomatoes, pan drippings, all manner of meat, fermented fish sauce, or even a quick grate of ginger. Here I call for collards, but you can substitute them with mustard or turnip greens. Either way, to serve this dish, place the braised greens on a family platter and the pickled stems in a bowl adjacent. That way, each diner can add as many pickled stems as they'd like, depending on whether they prefer buttery or tart flavors. You can also try swapping out the rosemary for another herb (like thyme, tarragon, or epazote) or tweaking the pickling liquid to include a spicy flavor (like an uncut whole serrano or Scotch bonnet pepper).

SERVES 4

Braised Collards

1 pound (about 2 bunches) collard greens

2 tablespoons neutral cooking oil

¼ yellow onion, grated on the small holes of a box grater

3 garlic cloves, grated on the small holes of a box grater

1 sprig rosemary

1½ teaspoons kosher salt

1 tablespoon apple cider vinegar

Pickled Stems

1 garlic clove, peeled and crushed

½ cup apple cider vinegar

2 tablespoons honey (or agave nectar or maple syrup)

1 tablespoon salt

To make the braised collards: Cut the middle stem out of each collard green leaf, but do not discard. (The easiest way to do this is to place the shiny side of the leaf facing down with the rib pointed upward, then run a paring knife along each side of the stem, working toward the bottom.) Stack the leafy parts of the collards into four mounds. Roll each stack lengthwise, then cut them into ½-inch-thick ribbons. Cut all of the stems crosswise into ⅓-inch pieces.

In a large cast-iron skillet or pot with a lid, heat the oil over low heat. Add the grated onion and garlic and cook, stirring occasionally, until fragrant, about 5 minutes. Add the rosemary sprig and cook just until fragrant, about 2 minutes. Season with the salt,

continued

then add the leaves of the greens. I like to use tongs to integrate the onion, garlic, and rosemary into the dense leafy greens that can clump together. Let the greens wilt for about 4 minutes, then add 1 cup of water and increase the heat to medium-high. Once the greens bubble gently, add the apple cider vinegar and stir. Cover, lower the heat to medium, and cook until fork-tender, about 20 minutes, periodically stirring the greens and checking to make sure they aren't boiling vigorously.

Meanwhile, make the pickled stems: In a saucepan, combine the crushed garlic, vinegar, honey, salt, and 1½ cups of water and bring to a boil on high. Add in the stems and cook until just tender, about 5 minutes. Remove from the heat and pour into a small serving bowl.

Transfer the cooked collards and their juices to a large serving bowl, discard the rosemary, and serve with the pickled stems on the side.

DRY-FRIED GREEN BEANS

This recipe holds a certain special memory for me. Growing up, my family would celebrate birthdays, awards, or just life at a vegan Chinese restaurant in San Francisco. Dry-fried green beans were a must-have every time we went there. Something about escaping the cold of San Francisco and enjoying slightly charred green beans with stewed eggplant and fried rice was so comforting. I knew I wanted to re-create this recipe and hopefully share the comforting energy that comes with it.

Dry-frying is a classic technique that, despite its name, doesn't involve a completely dry pan but rather a pan with a very small amount of oil. Dry-frying takes moisture out of the ingredients and makes them crispy. I love to dry-fry my green beans because this technique gives the green beans a nice charred flavor without resulting in overcooked and listless green beans. Tien Tsin chiles are small, mild dried chiles that impart lots of smoky chile flavor. Depending on where you live, they can be hard to find, but I recommend going to stores specializing in Chinese foods, a spice shop, or substituting with another small dried pepper such as chile de arbol. Sichuan peppercorns can be found at most grocery stores, but if you have trouble finding them, a spice shop is a good place to look. The spices in this recipe are used to flavor the oil in the pan and indirectly infuse the green beans.

SERVES 4

3 cups (about 12 ounces) fresh green beans, ends trimmed

3 tablespoons neutral cooking oil, such as grapeseed or avocado

1 tablespoon Sichuan peppercorns

5 Tien Tsin chiles (or another small dried chile, such as chile de arbol), sliced into ⅓-inch rings (optional)

3 garlic cloves, minced

2 teaspoons fresh grated ginger

2 tablespoons light soy sauce

Use a colander and towel to make sure the green beans are as dry as possible, then cut them in half, so they're 2 to 3 inches long.

In a large sauté pan, add the oil and Sichuan peppercorns. Heat the pan over medium heat and toast the peppercorns for about 4 minutes, until they start to darken. With a spatula or large spoon, scoop the peppercorns out of the pan and discard. (Don't worry if you can't get every single one.)

continued

Add half of the green beans (or however many you can fit in one layer) to the infused oil in the pan. Cook, stirring occasionally, for about 6 minutes, until most of them start to soften, wrinkle, and lighten in color. Remove the green beans from the pan with tongs and put them in a bowl. Repeat with the rest of the green beans.

Once all of the green beans are cooked, put them all back in the pan together. Still on medium heat, cook the green beans until they start to brown, stirring occasionally, about 8 minutes. Add the chiles (if using) and the garlic and ginger. Once that distinct garlic-ginger aroma is in the air and the garlic has just started to brown, about 3 minutes, stir in the soy sauce. Take the pan off the heat and place the green beans in a serving bowl or on a plate.

CURRY CABBAGE STEAKS WITH THYME + RED PEPPER BUTTER

This recipe is inspired by steamed cabbage, also known as curry cabbage or even Jamaican cabbage. It's an example of how one dish may have several different names. That said, don't call it cabbage curry, as that is another dish entirely, from India and Pakistan! Any curry powder can work for this recipe, but Jamaican works the best. Jamaican curry powder can be found in Jamaican, Caribbean, or a variety of African grocery stores. Steamed cabbage usually includes flavorful ingredients such as thyme, red bell pepper, bok choy, carrots, Scotch bonnet peppers, onions, and garlic, steamed with a bit of water. It is something that my mom has made for as long as I can remember. I've eaten this my entire life and never get bored with it. When cooking this recipe, it is important to keep the cabbage steaks close together on the baking sheet so the loose leaves don't dry out or crisp up too much. This dish is best when the butter is placed on the cabbage when it's still warm from the oven. You'll have a little extra red pepper butter, which you can use for making omelets, biscuits, or in place of butter in a savory recipe, such as in the Mashed Potatoes with Jerk Gravy (page 90).

SERVES 6

1 red bell pepper

¼ cup neutral cooking oil, such as avocado or grapeseed

1 teaspoon Jamaican curry powder

Freshly ground black pepper

1 green cabbage (about 3 pounds), sliced crosswise into ⅔-inch-thick steaks

Fine sea salt

1 teaspoon thyme leaves, chopped

1 cup (2 sticks) butter, at room temperature

Preheat the oven to 450°F.

Place the red pepper on a baking sheet and roast for 20 minutes, until charred. Set aside to cool.

In a small bowl, whisk together the oil, Jamaican curry powder, and a few cracks of black pepper. With a pastry brush, lightly brush one side of each cabbage steak with the oil mixture. You'll want to use about half the oil. If you don't own a pastry brush, drizzle a little oil evenly over the steaks. Sprinkle each steak with salt, then place the steaks oil-side down onto a baking sheet. Brush the other sides evenly with the rest of the oil, and sprinkle with more salt. Place the cabbage in the oven and cook for 15 minutes, flip each steak over, and then cook for another 15 to 20 minutes, until the edges start to turn dark brown.

When the bell pepper is cool enough to handle, discard the seeds and stem. Place in a blender or food processor and blend until the pepper is only slightly chunky. Strain the blended pepper, discarding the liquid, but taking care not to press down on the pepper puree. In a small bowl, using a whisk, mix the pepper puree and chopped thyme into the butter. To serve, top each cabbage steak with about 1 tablespoon of butter. Any leftover butter can be stored, sealed, in the fridge for up to 2 weeks.

MASHED POTATOES WITH JERK GRAVY

This is the first recipe I developed for this book. Jerk seasoning is commonly used to season main dishes like chicken, tofu, salmon, and really anything in between. This recipe uses jerk seasoning in an unconventional way, to season gravy, that tastes great and lets you control the spiciness level. This gravy uses a French and Creole technique called a roux, which is common in a variety of Creole recipes, like gumbo. Roux is equal amounts of any type of fat mixed with all-purpose flour. The roux is then cooked over heat to add flavor and thickness to sauces. Roux can be left pale—that would be a white roux. The longer you cook the roux, the deeper in color it gets—from white, blond, brown, to dark roux. This recipe uses a brown roux, to act as a thickener and add a toasty flavor and deep color. Don't feel a need to rush this part, as the gravy is way less complicated than it can seem.

SERVES 4

Mashed Potatoes

2 pounds (5 or 6 medium) Russet potatoes, scrubbed, peeled, and cut crosswise into thirds

1½ teaspoons kosher salt

3 tablespoons extra-virgin olive oil

½ cup heavy cream

½ teaspoon freshly ground black pepper

Jerk Gravy

2 tablespoons all-purpose flour

2 teaspoons jerk seasoning (page 210)

2 tablespoons unsalted butter

1 teaspoon fresh thyme leaves (from about 3 sprigs), chopped

1 garlic clove, crushed

½ teaspoon fine sea salt

Make the potatoes: Bring a stockpot of water to a boil over high heat. Add the potatoes and 1 teaspoon of the salt and boil until tender, about 13 minutes.

While your potatoes are boiling, start on the jerk gravy. In a saucepan over medium-low heat, toast the flour and jerk seasoning, stirring until the jerk seasoning is fragrant, about 2 minutes. Add the butter and allow it to melt. Stir with a wooden spoon, making sure all of the flour is combined with the butter. Whisk in the thyme, garlic, and salt, and then slowly add 1 cup of water. Once combined, take the pan off the heat and let the gravy thicken while you switch back to the potatoes.

When the potatoes are tender, drain them while reserving ¼ cup of the starchy cooking water. Transfer the drained potatoes to a bowl and use a large spoon to fold in the olive oil; the potatoes should slightly break apart. With a slotted metal spoon, wooden spoon, or potato masher, smash the potatoes incrementally while adding in the heavy cream, remaining ½ teaspoon of salt, and pepper.

Once the potatoes are mashed to your liking (I like mine thick with small chunks), drizzle in the reserved starchy water and mix. Place the gravy over medium heat and gently warm for about 4 minutes. Transfer the mashed potatoes to a serving dish and pour the gravy into a separate bowl to serve on the side.

WHOLE ROASTED SWEET POTATOES WITH CANELA GINGER CRUMBLE

Sweet potatoes are cooked so differently around the world. When it comes to my family, we have at least three different types of sweet potato recipes. My extended family would serve sweet potatoes in orange zest, cinnamon, and sugar syrup for Thanksgiving. In my house, we love to cook them whole, split them open, and flavor them with brown sugar, cinnamon, butter, and thyme. There's something so glorious about taking a hot sweet potato out of the oven practically melting with reduced, naturally sugary caramel. Once you cut open the roasted sweet potato, the sweet and earthy aroma fills the air.

SERVES 4

2 medium sweet potatoes, scrubbed and dried

2 tablespoons unsalted butter, at room temperature

½ cup all-purpose flour

½ cup firmly packed light brown sugar

1 tablespoon grated ginger

¼ cup chopped pecans

½ teaspoon salt

1 teaspoon ground cinnamon

1 teaspoon ground nutmeg

1 teaspoon grated lemon zest

Preheat the oven to 425°F. Place the sweet potatoes on a parchment paper–lined baking sheet and roast, until soft when pierced with a fork, for 45 minutes to an hour. You'll know the sweet potatoes are done if you start smelling a brown-sugary aroma or notice the skin crinkle, with sugary liquid running out.

While the potatoes are baking, in a small bowl, combine the butter, flour, sugar, ginger, pecans, salt, cinnamon, nutmeg, and lemon zest and mix together with your hands or a fork. The mixture should look sandy with small chunks of butter.

Slit the cooked sweet potatoes in half lengthwise and return them to the baking sheet. Spoon the topping evenly onto each half. Bake at 425°F on the oven's top rack for 20 minutes, or until the crumble looks golden brown and smells toasty. Let cool for 4 minutes and enjoy!

FRIJOLES NEGROS

This recipe is a lesson in simmering. Simmering—when a liquid is hot and lightly bubbling but not boiling—is such an important technique. It ensures that the dish you're cooking gets saturated with flavor without scorching or overcooking the ingredients. Frijoles negros is an everyday sort of dish that can be found throughout the Spanish-speaking world, in what we call North America, the Caribbean, and Central and South America. I love the common addition of tomatoes, but in this recipe I wanted to keep it simple and focus on the rich umami of black beans. If you would like to add tomatoes, any variety such as heirloom, Roma, beefsteak, or even cherry will work. Just cut the tomatoes into chunky pieces, squeeze out any seeds and jellylike bits (save for compost or broth), and add them when you add the water to the pan. Serve with rice, a fried egg, or on its own.

SERVES 4 TO 6

2 tablespoons neutral cooking oil, such as avocado or grapeseed

½ small sweet onion, finely diced

1 red bell pepper, finely diced

2 garlic cloves, minced

1 teaspoon ground cumin

1 teaspoon dried oregano

2 teaspoons fine sea salt

2 (15-ounce) cans black beans, rinsed and drained, or 1 pound dried black beans, cooked

1 cup vegetable broth or water

Freshly ground black pepper

Fresh cilantro leaves for garnish

Heat a 10-inch cast-iron skillet or a saucepan over medium heat and combine the oil, onion, and bell pepper. Cover and cook for 10 minutes, stirring occasionally, until softened. Add the garlic, cumin, oregano, and salt and cook, uncovered, for 5 more minutes, until the garlic and peppers are browned on the edges. Add the drained beans to the pan and cook for 5 additional minutes. A few of the beans will break down, helping create the gravy-like texture.

Add the water and simmer, covered, for 10 minutes, stirring about halfway through. Finally, remove the lid and let simmer for 10 more minutes, or until most of the liquid has reduced, stirring periodically to make sure the bottom doesn't burn. Season with black pepper and top with cilantro, then serve. Store any leftovers in an airtight container in the fridge for up to 1 week.

CREAMY REFRIED BEANS

I love this recipe because it can be eaten with traditional Mexican dishes such as Arroz Rojo (opposite) and mole poblano, as a side dish in any meal, or as a delicious meal by itself with a couple of fresh tortillas, Salsa Molcajete Roja (page 64), and some avocado slices. Frijoles de la olla are when the pinto beans are just left whole. My mom will usually cook a big pot on a Sunday, then over the course of the week use them in different ways—mixed with a bit of salsa and scooped up with a corn tortilla for lunch, as a chili component, or as a nachos topping. By Thursday, she will freeze what is left in two-cup amounts for later meals.

I try to buy organic beans and from local farmers, but canned beans work nicely in this recipe as well. Naturally, the flavor will be more infused if the beans are cooked from scratch. I find the technique of boiling the beans, letting them sit, and then cooking them makes the beans cook faster.

SERVES 6

2 cups dried pinto beans, preferably organic, rinsed

1 teaspoon fine sea salt (plus more as needed)

3 tablespoons neutral cooking oil

½ yellow onion, coarsely chopped

½ green bell pepper, coarsely chopped

3 garlic cloves, coarsely chopped

1 teaspoon ground cumin

Freshly ground black pepper

In a stockpot, add the beans, salt, and enough water to fully submerge the beans. Turn the heat on high, let the beans come to a boil, then turn off the heat and cover for 1 hour. Drain and rinse the beans, then add them back into the pot with 6 cups of water, or enough so that the beans are submerged by about 2 inches. Bring to a boil, then decrease to medium-low heat for 60 to 80 minutes. Test to make sure the beans are fully cooked by tasting a bean. You'll know they're done when the bean is soft and not gritty or dry on the inside. Drain the beans and set aside.

In the same pot you cooked the beans, heat the oil over medium-low heat. Add the onion, bell pepper, garlic, and cumin and cook for about 10 minutes, stirring occasionally, until the vegetables are soft. Stir in the beans, then transfer the mixture to a blender. Blend, gradually increasing the speed from low to high, for around 2 minutes or until smooth, making sure to stir in intervals by turning off the blender and using a spoon or blender attachment. Return the beans to the pot, and warm for 5 minutes on medium-low. Season with salt and black pepper.

ARROZ ROJO

This recipe pairs great with Creamy Refried Beans (opposite). For arroz rojo, I find that long-grain white rice is essential: Brown rice will take four times longer to cook, and short-grain rice may soften too quickly. This rice recipe is from my Abuelita Velia, who claims you need a special touch for the best arroz rojo. I think the special touch she is referring to is patience and attentiveness. I tweaked her recipe a bit to be foolproof. If you are already familiar with red rice or jollof, then you already know this technique, which originated in Africa and, in this instance, was carried to Mexico and the United States through the tremendous African influence in Spanish cuisine. The technique largely rests on steaming rice in a tomato-umami-rich broth. While jollof and red rice may sometimes use powdered crayfish or shrimp and other complex smoky ingredients, it isn't usually common in Mexican American arroz rojo preparation. If you have the opportunity to use Mexican oregano, I highly recommend it for a bit more complex flavor. This recipe works great as long as the heat is not turned up too high.

SERVES 4 TO 6

1 cup long-grain white rice

2 tablespoons neutral cooking oil, such as avocado or grapeseed

1½ cups low-sodium chicken broth

½ cup tomato sauce

1 teaspoon fine sea salt

2 teaspoons dried oregano

Place the rice in a strainer and rinse until the water runs clear. Set aside to drain. In a 10-inch skillet, heat the oil over medium-high heat. Add the rice and toast, stirring occasionally (I like to use a wooden spoon), for about 10 minutes, until most of the rice is a tan color. The rice should not char but will smell toasty. Add the broth, tomato sauce, salt, and oregano and stir gently to combine. Cover, decrease the heat to low, and simmer for 10 minutes. Uncover to scrape the bottom of the pan, then re-cover and simmer for 10 more minutes. Take the rice off the heat and let it sit uncovered for 5 minutes before serving.

COCONUT RICE + PEAS

Historians have traced this dish to the Akan people of West Africa, and its original name is waakye. The beans used are often black-eyed peas. It has a variety of expressions and is also known as ayimolou in Togo. It goes by cook-up rice in Guyana and rice and peas in Jamaica, the Bahamas, and Barbados. "Peas" refers to the gungo pea bean, also known as the pigeon pea. Restaurants nowadays often sub kidney beans, and I've seen my mom use adzuki beans. She claims adzukis are most similar to the gungo pea, as they are sweeter than the kidney bean. What I love most about this recipe is the rice. Rice has the ability to soak up all the flavors of spices, coconut milk, and whatever you serve on top of it. This recipe is most similar to the Jamaican version, which is known to hold up well against gravylike liquids from jerk, escoveitch, and brown stew.

SERVES 4 TO 6

2 tablespoons neutral cooking oil, such as grapeseed

⅔ cup jasmine rice, rinsed until the water runs clear

½ small onion, finely diced

2 teaspoons fresh thyme leaves

1 teaspoon fine sea salt

1 cup low-sodium chicken broth

⅔ cup red kidney beans

1 habanero pepper, left whole with the stem

¼ cup coconut milk

In a 10-inch skillet, heat the oil over medium-high heat. Add the rice and cook, stirring occasionally, for about 1 minute, until the rice is coated in oil. The rice should not brown at all. Add the onion, thyme, and salt. Cook for another minute—the rice should still not be browned. Add the broth, beans, habanero, and coconut milk and stir to gently combine. Cover and let simmer on very low heat for 15 minutes, then stir again, making sure to reach to the bottom of the pan. Cover and simmer for 10 more minutes. Take the rice off the heat, remove the habanero, and let sit uncovered for 5 minutes before serving.

SHORBA ADAS (RED LENTIL SOUP)

Shorba means "soup" in Arabic, and as I was developing this recipe, I thought of the many variations I've experienced—some with an herbaceous finishing oil, others with lemons or oranges as garnish, or with tomato puree and spinach—from places such as Palestine, Egypt, and Jordan. Lentils are believed to be the first cultivated legume, and so many medicinal traditions have a healing soup or other use related to lentils. While it is a superquick recipe to make, shorba always makes me feel like I'm having a comfy dinner with family. I have so many memories of weeknight dinners when my mom would have a pot of shorba cooking on the stove while we unwound from a long day. She would serve this soup with a few pieces of warmed goodness, varying from freshly bought pita to a warm corn tortilla to buttered sourdough. This fragrant soup sits at a table steaming, sending the scents of cooked veggies, garlic, and cumin into the air. I highly recommend serving this with the Herby Infused Oil and a squeeze of lemon juice to bring the flavors all together. One thing I see as a unification of so many cultures is the presence of green and orange produce (in this case, green bell pepper and carrot) in a dish. It is an example of the brilliance of so many indigenous cultures because this combination increases the body's uptake of calcium by a vast percentage. It is the Black culinary expression of collard greens served with sweet potatoes, the occasional green peas and carrots in Mexican arroz rojo, and the cabbage and carrots in Jamaican steamed cabbage. There are so many more examples, and every time I see one, I see unity.

SERVES 4 TO 6

1 green bell pepper, cut into pea-size dice

1 medium carrot, cut into pea-size dice

2 tablespoons extra-virgin olive oil

3 garlic cloves, minced

2 teaspoons fine sea salt

1 teaspoon ground cumin

1 cup red lentils, rinsed and picked through

6 cups vegetable broth

1 lemon, cut into wedges for serving

Herby Infused Oil (page 203) for serving (optional)

continued

Heat a stockpot over medium heat and add the bell pepper, carrot, and olive oil. Cook for 6 minutes, stirring occasionally, until aromatic. Stir in the garlic, salt, and cumin, and cook for 2 more minutes. Add the lentils and broth and bring to a boil over high heat. This will take 10 to 15 minutes, depending on the strength of your stove.

Lower the heat to medium and let simmer for about 40 minutes, stirring occasionally, until the soup looks rich and cloudy. Serve in bowls with a squeeze of lemon juice and drizzle of infused oil, if desired.

DUNGENESS CRAB TINOLA

Tinola or tinolang is a hearty, delicious soup that comes from the Philippines. Tinola is normally a light but rich broth that incorporates the flavors of fresh vegetables, aromatics like ginger and garlic, and umami flavor from a dash of fish sauce. Tinolang manok (chicken tinola) has a long, celebrated existence, but this recipe swaps the chicken for Dungeness crab. The Dungeness crab can absorb all the fragrant flavors in the broth, and it has a sweeter taste than other kinds of crab. Dungeness crabs also have a thinner shell compared with a common crab you might find at a grocery store or fish market. I find the thin shells are helpful when cleaning the crabs and making stocks. (If you don't have access to fresh Dungeness crab or the time to break down a whole crab, substituting prepackaged crabmeat and vegetable broth for the crab and crab stock works just as well.) Malunggay (also called moringa) leaves are a great traditional addition to this soup; they are soft and earthy leaves that, for this recipe, should be whole and not powdered or dried. Malunggay can be found in Filipino-owned markets (check the frozen section). If you're having a hard time finding malunggay, go ahead and leave it out. Although I have never had a problem, chayote can be a temporary skin irritant for some. I recommend handling carefully or with gloves.

SERVES 4 TO 6

2 tablespoons neutral cooking oil, such as avocado or grapeseed

3 garlic cloves, minced

½ yellow onion, sliced into ¼-inch-thick half-moons

2 teaspoons grated ginger

6 cups crab stock (page 206), seafood stock, or veggie stock (page 205)

2 tablespoons fish sauce (plus 1 tablespoon if you're using vegetable stock)

1 baby bok choy, cut into 1-inch pieces

1 chayote, halved, seeded, and then cut crosswise into thirds

2 tablespoons malunggay leaves, fresh or frozen (optional)

1 teaspoon fine sea salt

Meat from 1 cooked and cleaned Dungeness crab (about 2 pounds; see page 207) or 1½ cups (about ¾ pound) lump crabmeat

In a stockpot, add the oil and heat over medium heat. Then add the garlic, onion, and ginger. Sauté, stirring occasionally, until the onion is translucent, about 5 minutes. Add the stock and fish sauce. Cover the pot with a lid and bring to a gentle simmer. Add the bok choy, chayote, malunggay (if using), and the salt. Adjust the heat to maintain a gentle simmer, and cook uncovered for 5 minutes. Add the crabmeat. Turn the heat to low and cook for 5 more minutes, so the flavors may infuse. Serve immediately, or store in an airtight container in the fridge for up to 4 days.

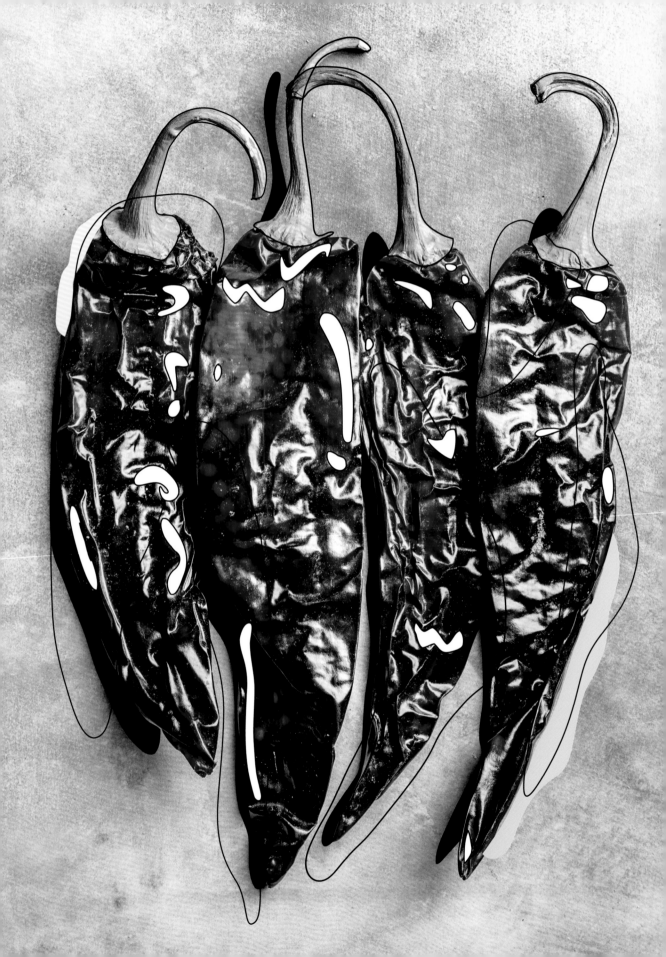

SUNDAY DINNER
MENU INSPIRATION

Whole Roasted Sweet Potato with
Canela Ginger Crumble (page 92)

+

Cornflour Panfried Fish (page 133)

+

Braised Collards with Pickled Stems
(page 83)

+

Corn Cakes (page 37)

+

Jamaica + Pineapple Punch
(page 180)

Mains —— 4

When working in a fine dining restaurant, I wake up early in the morning and spend hours helping to prep for dinner service. Dinner service is almost like a performance when all the cooks and chefs in the kitchen combine the different components and dishes that they've worked on all day to make a delicious, memorable meal for the diners. There are so many people involved in prepping and cooking, along with an entire team that is cleaning and washing dishes. Fortunately, we don't need a full staff and ten hours to create a great personal meal service. In this chapter, I was very intentional about offering mains that are not too overwhelming in heaviness *or* effort. If you're looking for a lighter dish that includes lots of flavor, try out the Mole Verde Maitake Mushroom Tacos (page 122), Miser Wot (Red Lentil Stew; page 117), or the Whole Roasted Lemon Pepper Chicken (page 139) with a salad. If you want a heartier dish, I recommend the Dakgangjeong (Korean Fried Chicken) and Chard Cabbage Slaw (page 135), or the Makawoni au Graten (page 125) with the Green Zesty Salad (page 79). You might recognize the Ribeye Tostada with Squash Medallions and Creamy Beans (page 141) from my television appearances—I changed it a bit to make it more workable for the home kitchen.

CREOLE MUSHROOM HAND PIES

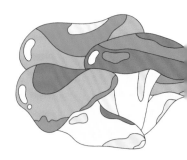

As the family cook who wants to please everyone, I am faced with serious challenges. I'm an omnivore now, but I was raised (for the most part) vegetarian. My comfort foods are still vegetarian and vegan dishes. My sisters Fidela, eighteen, and Su, nineteen, are devoted to a plant-based lifestyle. They do not waver (though I remember Su eating meat when she was younger and teasing us for choosing not to eat it!). But, even the vegans in my house can't agree on what they'll eat. If there is a superhealthy stereotype of a vegan, that is Fidela! She loves stuff like raw foods, kombucha, and fresh veggies. Su, on the other hand, enjoys vegan interpretations of popular meat dishes she gets at restaurants and grocery stores in NYC, where she goes to school. They have always been similar yet polar opposites, those two. For example, they both are dedicated to the arts and moved nearly three thousand miles away from home, from California to NYC, only to live in the same neighborhood as each other. Su is an acting student at NYU's Tisch School of the Arts, while Fidela is a stylish fashion design student at The New School's Parsons School of Design. When they visit home, I think about recipes that will please them both. I recently re-created the yummy oyster-filled hand pies I fell in love with when I visited Louisiana. I love the umami of oysters and thought a great substitute would be a creole mushroom filling. I spent a long time figuring out how to add flavor and color to the crust without overworking the dough. The technique I settled on produces a refined, crisp crust with a hint of tomato that tastes like it requires hours of time (it doesn't!).

MAKES 12 PIES

Pie Crust

1½ cups all-purpose flour

¼ teaspoon fine sea salt

½ cup shortening

1 tablespoon tomato paste (optional)

Mushroom Filling

2 tablespoons neutral cooking oil, such as avocado or grapeseed

½ diced yellow onion

½ cup diced celery stalk

½ cup diced green bell pepper

1½ cups thinly sliced mushroom caps

1 bunch Swiss chard, stemmed and thinly sliced

1 garlic clove, minced

½ teaspoon paprika

½ teaspoon fresh thyme

½ teaspoon creole seasoning (page 209)

continued

To make the pie crust: In a medium bowl, whisk together the flour and salt. Add the shortening and cut the flour and shortening into each other (with a fork in one hand and knife in the other, as if you are cutting an imaginary sandwich into tiny bites), until the dough forms little pea-size balls. Drizzle ½ cup water into the flour and shortening mixture bit by bit and gently mix with a rubber spatula until it is combined into a soft dough. If desired, transfer ¼ cup of the dough to a small bowl and add the tomato paste. Mix with a fork until combined, then add it back to the rest of the dough and gently incorporate with your hands until the tomato paste dough is marbled into the plain dough (take care not to overwork). Cover dough with a kitchen towel or lid and set aside.

To make the mushroom filling: Heat a sauté pan over medium heat and add the oil, onion, celery, and bell pepper. Sauté until the onion is nearly translucent and the bell pepper is softened, about 8 minutes. Add the mushrooms, Swiss chard, garlic, paprika, thyme, and creole seasoning and sauté, stirring occasionally, until all of the ingredients are cooked down and the onion and mushrooms are caramelized, 3 to 5 minutes. Transfer the mixture to a bowl.

Preheat the oven to 350°F. Line a baking sheet with parchment paper. On a floured work surface, roll out the dough as thin as possible without creating any holes, applying even, gentle pressure. Using a 3-inch floured circle cutter, cut the dough into twenty-four circles and lay twelve of them on the prepared baking sheet. Spoon ¼ cup of the vegetable filling onto each of the twelve dough circles, then place the remaining twelve dough circles on top. Use a fork to gently press the edges together just enough so they adhere. Using a paring knife, cut an X on the top layer of dough for each hand pie.

Bake for 10 to 15 minutes, until the pie crust is slightly brown and firm. Let cool for a few minutes before serving.

TRINITY KOROKKE

Korokke, potato croquettes that are a popular Japanese street food, are great as an appetizer or even for breakfast or brunch. I developed this recipe for NBCU Upfronts, a red-carpet event held at Radio City Music Hall that raises millions of dollars by showcasing the upcoming shows and selling the advertising space. Basically, all the network stars attend, and it is a preview of the next season of programming. My assignment was to create a one- or two-bite breakfast item that could be easily eaten on the red carpet. I intentionally wanted something that wouldn't make a mess. Also, I had to consider that people would be eating these bites while getting interviewed. The Trinity Korokke was an overwhelming hit! Now that I don't have to worry about celebs eating these on the red carpet without disturbing their makeup, I've made a few changes: I added diced bell pepper and onion to give the creamy mashed potatoes more texture, and mozzarella to create a gooey cheese pull.

MAKES 8 TO 12 CROQUETTES

1 pound Russet potatoes, peeled and cut into 1-inch pieces

2 celery stalks, diced

½ yellow onion, diced

1 small green bell pepper, diced

1 teaspoon fine sea salt

½ teaspoon freshly ground black pepper

1 cup all-purpose flour

2 cups panko bread crumbs

2 eggs

1 tablespoon Kewpie mayonnaise

2 tablespoons milk, any kind

1 cup shredded mozzarella

½ cup neutral cooking oil, such as grapeseed, plus more as needed

Katsu sauce or ketchup for serving (optional)

Bring a large saucepan of water to a boil. Cook the potatoes for 10 minutes, or until tender. Add the celery, onion, and bell pepper and boil for 4 more minutes. The veggies will be lightly boiled but still have a crisp bite. Drain the contents of the pan, transfer to a large bowl, and mash the vegetable mixture together with a large spoon, ideally a slotted spoon or a potato masher. (The celery, onion, and bell pepper will retain their shape.) Add the salt and black pepper, then chill in the fridge for 15 minutes, or until cool enough to handle.

continued

While the potato mixture is cooling, prepare your dredging station. In a shallow bowl, combine the flour and panko. In a separate bowl, whisk together the eggs, mayo, and milk.

Remove the potato mixture from the fridge and stir in the shredded mozzarella. Scoop out ¼-cup portions of the mixture and shape into discs. Dip each disc into the wet dredging mixture, then the dry mixture, ensuring each disc is evenly coated.

In a large skillet, heat the oil over medium heat until it is shimmering. Working in batches so as not to crowd the pan, fry the croquettes for 2 to 3 minutes on each side, until golden brown. Repeat this with the rest of the croquettes, adding more oil to the pan as needed so that the oil reaches halfway up the croquettes. Serve immediately with katsu sauce or ketchup for dipping, if desired.

YACHAEJEON (VEGETABLE PANCAKES) WITH CHO GANJANG

Yachaejeon and buchimgae are two common types of savory Korean pancakes. The main difference is that buchimgae has eggs and yachaejeon doesn't. I find that yachaejeon gets crispier and takes less time to cook than buchimgae. This dish works for new and experienced cooks alike and even with younger children (I've taught this recipe to people as young as seven!). I think the colorful veggies are really interesting to children and helps encourage them to try different ingredients at a young age. It doesn't require a lot of stirring, and once the pancake browns the flip is pretty straightforward. I recommend using a stainless-steel or nonstick skillet for the yachaejeon, as the batter tends to stick to cast-iron pans. A tip to get the pancakes crispier is to lift them from the pan only when it's time to flip them. Make sure to pair these with the soy-and-vinegar-based cho ganjang dipping sauce!

MAKES 8 PANCAKES

Cho Ganjang

2 tablespoons soy sauce

2 tablespoons distilled white vinegar

1 garlic clove, crushed

2 teaspoons toasted sesame seeds

1 green onion, green parts only, thinly sliced crosswise

Yachaejeon

1 red bell pepper, cut lengthwise into ⅛-inch-thick slices

1 green onion, green parts only, cut into 1-inch pieces

1 bunch green or rainbow chard, stemmed and thinly sliced (about 2 cups)

½ cup all-purpose flour

2 tablespoons neutral cooking oil, plus more as needed

First, make the cho ganjang: In a small bowl, whisk together the soy sauce, vinegar, garlic, sesame seeds, green onion, and 2 tablespoons of water and let sit for at least 10 minutes while you make the pancakes.

To make the yachaejeon: Cut the bell pepper slices in half crosswise. In a large bowl, combine the bell pepper, green onion, and chard.

continued

In a separate bowl, whisk together the flour and ½ cup of water. It should have a thin, pancake batter consistency. Pour the batter over the chard mixture. There will be barely enough batter to coat the vegetables.

Line a plate with paper towels or set a cooling rack over a baking sheet. Use a stainless-steel or nonstick pan that is at least 10 inches wide and place it over medium-high heat. Add the oil. Once the oil is hot, use a ⅓-cup measuring cup to scoop the batter into the pan, forming evenly sized pancakes. Cook four pancakes at a time. Flatten the pancakes with a spatula and cook for 4 minutes on each side, until slightly golden. Drain the cooked pancakes on the prepared plate or baking sheet. Repeat with the remaining batter, adding a little more oil to the pan if it looks dry. Serve with the cho ganjang on the side for dipping.

MISER WOT (RED LENTIL STEW)

Miser wot is a stew that originated in Ethiopia. Wot is a type of stew that can take on so many different forms and can contain chicken, fish, mushrooms, eggplant, or, in this case, red lentils. In most wots, there is niter kibbeh, a clarified butter seasoned with herbs and spices, and a reddish hue from a berbere spice mixture. While berbere can be found in grocery stores, I recommend making it at home (see page 211)—or supporting local spice shops, a fair-trade producer, or an Ethiopian-owned grocery store. Miser wot is usually vegan or vegetarian and full of amazing flavors of caramelized onion, toasty spices, garlic, and simmered tomato, all mingling with soft lentils. It is most traditionally served with a bread called injera, which is made using a long sourdough-like process that requires fermenting and feeding the starter over the course of almost a week. It's a little hard to find in stores—but you can pick it up from Ethiopian and Eritrean restaurants that make fresh injera. There are fewer than four hundred Ethiopian and Eritrean restaurants in the US, and it is important to support the food traditions that Ethiopian and Eritrean restaurant owners bring to the world.

SERVES 4 TO 6

2 tablespoons extra-virgin olive oil

1 sweet yellow onion, finely diced

¼ cup Berbere Seasoning (page 211)

4 garlic cloves, minced

2 tablespoons tomato paste

2½ teaspoons fine sea salt

2 cups red lentils, rinsed

Injera for serving

In a large saucepan with a lid, heat the olive oil over medium heat and add the onion. Cook the onion, covered, for 15 minutes, stirring every 5 minutes until the onions are golden and caramelized. Adjust the heat as needed to prevent burning. Uncover the pan, add the berbere, garlic, tomato paste, and salt and stir to mix thoroughly. Decrease the heat to low and cook for about 5 minutes, until the mixture looks like a deep red paste with a few visible onion pieces.

continued

Add the lentils and 3 cups of water, increase the heat to high, cover the pan, and bring to a simmer. Lower the heat to maintain a hardy simmer and cook for 15 minutes. You will see some of the water reducing. Be sure to adjust the heat as needed to maintain a steady simmer. Uncover the pan and cook on low, scraping the bottom of the pan continuously, for 10 minutes, until the lentils are soft but still hold their shape. The lentils will look reddish brown. Take the pan off the heat, cover, and allow to cool for 5 minutes. Serve with injera.

JERK EGGPLANT STEAKS

Jerk seasoning is commonly found on chicken, but it can be used on just about any ingredient. Jerk has a wonderful, toasty, spiced flavor. This recipe uses jerk butter to infuse flavor into the eggplant. You'll probably have leftover butter, and I love to use jerk butter on toast, popcorn, or to cook vegetables like Swiss chard. I've also seen it used as a finish on a beef steak. I think the possibilities are endless.

SERVES 4 TO 6

½ cup (1 stick) unsalted butter, at room temperature, plus more as needed

3 tablespoons jerk seasoning (page 210)

1 globe eggplant (about 1 pound) cut lengthwise into ½-inch-thick slices

Sea salt

Coconut Rice and Peas (page 98) or cooked rice for serving

In a bowl, mash together the butter and jerk seasoning with a fork until the seasoning is evenly incorporated. Crosshatch the eggplant slices by gently scoring the flesh diagonally with a knife, making sure not to cut through all the way, until you get a diamond pattern. Score both sides of the slices except for the two pieces that have skin on one side (in this case, only score the flesh side).

With a butter knife, spread a thin layer of the jerk butter on both sides of the eggplant slices. (Store any leftover butter, sealed, in the fridge for up to 1 week. Use jerk butter for toasts, searing, or when roasting veggies and meats such as chicken.)

Heat a large skillet over medium heat. Brown the eggplant steaks until soft and golden, about 6 minutes on each side. If the eggplant starts to stick to the pan, add a little butter and then gently free it with a spatula. Sprinkle the steaks with salt and serve with the coconut rice or your favorite rice.

MOLE VERDE MAITAKE MUSHROOM TACOS

Maitake mushrooms (also known as Grifola frondosa, dancing mushroom, and hen of the woods) are great for this taco filling recipe because they hold their shape really well, absorb a ton of flavor, and get a superyummy caramelization on the outside. I find that most mushrooms contain a lot of water, but maitakes do not seem to release so much water when cooked. If you can't find maitakes, you can swap in slices of oyster mushrooms or whatever you have available instead. Similarly, this recipe suggests a certain mushroom size, but feel free to prepare the mushrooms however big or small you want. I don't specify how you should clean your mushrooms because I know different cultures approach this task differently. I grew up around people who soak or quickly rinse mushrooms with water, while others use a dry brush to wipe away debris. You'll end up with a lot of leftover mole, which I have found can go on any vegetable, especially eggplant and cauliflower, or even tofu. You can also use it to coat tortillas and then fry them (the term *enchilada* comes from the indigenous Mexican tradition of coating a tortilla in a chile sauce and then searing—or not—before eating). And if you don't feel like making tacos, the mushrooms work great on their own with rice and beans.

SERVES 4 TO 6

1 pound tomatillos, husks removed

4 garlic cloves, unpeeled

1 yellow onion, quartered, with the skin on

1 serrano pepper

2 teaspoons fine sea salt

½ lime, juiced

½ cup packed fresh cilantro leaves and stems

Leaves from 2 sprigs fresh oregano or ½ teaspoon dried oregano

½ cup toasted hulled sunflower seeds

½ teaspoon ground cumin

8 ounces maitake mushrooms, cleaned (see Cook's Note) and torn into 2-inch pieces

3 tablespoons neutral cooking oil, such as grapeseed or avocado

Corn tortillas (page 213) or store-bought for serving

Sliced avocado for serving (optional)

Escabeche (page 217) for serving (optional)

Salsa Molcajete Roja (page 64) for serving (optional)

continued

Preheat the oven to 450°F. Lightly oil a baking sheet and add the tomatillos, garlic, onion, and serrano pepper. Roast for 15 minutes, until the onion looks charred on the bottom. Let cool slightly.

When cool enough to handle, remove the skins from the garlic and onion. Cut the serrano down the middle, carefully scoop out the seeds, and discard the seeds and stem. Place all the roasted ingredients into a blender with the salt, lime juice, cilantro, oregano, sunflower seeds, cumin, and ½ cup of water. Blend the mole until smooth.

Place the mushrooms in a bowl and pour enough mole over them to coat them entirely. Cover the bowl and let them marinate for 20 minutes. Warm tortillas by wrapping 8 tortillas in aluminum foil and place in a preheated oven at 325°F for 20 to 25 minutes. The oven method is slower than the microwave, but it provides a gentler heating that allows the tortillas to steam. You can also reheat them on the stove top straight on the burner or in a lightly greased pan on low heat in batches.

To cook the mushrooms, heat the oil in a cast-iron skillet over medium heat. Pick up a piece of mushroom, allowing the excess mole to fall away into the bowl and wiping off excess sauce if necessary. (Excess mole may steam the mushrooms, and we are looking for the rich caramelization of a hearty sear.) Working in batches as needed so as not to crowd the pan, sear the mushrooms for 2 to 3 minutes on each side, until the edges are light brown. Once you smell the smoky sear, transfer the mushrooms to a serving dish. Serve alongside the warm tortillas with your favorite toppings and encourage your guests to make tacos at the table. Leftover mole can be stored in a sealed container in the fridge for up to 1 week.

Cook's Note: Clean maitake mushrooms using your preferred method. I like to gently remove the soil from the mushrooms in a bowl of water and pat dry with a towel. Tear the cleaned mushrooms into pieces about the width of 3 or 4 fingers.

MAKAWONI AU GRATEN

Many cultures throughout the world have their own macaroni dish. I like the Jamaican macaroni that is boiled in chicken broth and the Trinidadian version that is so thick it can be sliced like a pie, hence the name macaroni pie. In Egypt, it is called macaroni béchamel and sometimes contains a thin layer of ground beef. In the United States, we have Chef James Hemings, an immensely talented Black man, to thank for introducing macaroni and cheese (and specifically, the technique of boiling the pasta in milk). I present here the Haitian version, which is usually made with rigatoni. My spin on it uses French, Italian, and Dutch cheeses, but the complex flavor is pure Haitian deliciousness.

SERVES 6

1 pound dried rigatoni

2 tablespoons unsalted butter

½ white onion, cut into ¼-inch dice

½ red bell pepper, cut into ¼-inch dice

1 teaspoon sea salt

½ teaspoon freshly ground black pepper

6 ounces Parmesan, shredded on a box grater (about 1½ cups)

6 ounces Gruyère, shredded on a box grater (about 1½ cups)

5 ounces Gouda, shredded on a box grater (about 1½ cups)

1 (12-ounce) can evaporated milk, preferably organic

In a stockpot, bring about 2 quarts of salted water to a boil over high heat. Boil the pasta until al dente, about 12 minutes, then drain and rinse with cool running water. Set to the side.

Preheat the oven to 350°F and grease a 9 by 13-inch baking pan.

Dry the stockpot, then, over medium heat, add the butter, onion, bell pepper, salt, and black pepper. Sauté for 5 minutes, or until soft. Turn off the heat and add the drained pasta. Toss the pasta so it is evenly coated with the bell pepper and onion. Add 1 cup of the Parmesan, 1 cup of the Gruyère, and 1 cup of the Gouda, and toss the pasta. While still tossing, slowly add the evaporated milk.

Transfer the cheesy pasta mixture into the prepared baking pan. Tightly cover with aluminum foil and bake for 30 minutes. Remove the foil and sprinkle the remaining cheese on top of the pasta. Place the baking pan back into the oven and cook, uncovered, until the cheese melts, about 10 minutes. Allow the pasta to cool slightly before serving.

FARMERS' MARKET CARBONARA

I love this recipe because most of the ingredients can be found at the farmers' market. Classic carbonara is a very simple recipe that requires only a few ingredients: pasta, pancetta, cheese, and eggs. So getting the best quality ingredients available is important. I like to pick up eggs, fresh pasta, eggplant, and edible blossoms or flowers at our local farmers' market to make this version. This pasta recipe is super rich, so I recommend enjoying it with a refreshing drink like the Sun Chai on page 190 and the Quick Green Zesty Salad on page 79. If you can't find fresh pasta, use about 8 ounces of dry organic pasta and boil it for an additional 4 to 5 minutes.

SERVES 4

2 eggs

½ cup grated Pecorino Romano, plus more for topping

Freshly ground black pepper

1 Chinese eggplant or ½ globe eggplant (about 9 ounces)

1 tablespoon all-purpose flour

1 tablespoon cornstarch

½ cup neutral cooking oil, such as avocado or grapeseed, plus more as needed

Sea salt

12 ounces fresh spaghetti or other fresh pasta

Edible blossoms or flowers for serving (optional)

Fill a stockpot with enough salted water to cover the pasta and bring to a boil. In a small bowl, whisk together the eggs, ½ cup of Pecorino Romano, and 1 teaspoon of pepper. Set this to the side.

In a large bowl, combine the flour and the cornstarch and set aside. On a cutting board, peel the eggplant. If you're using a Chinese eggplant, cut it crosswise into ¼-inch-thick medallions, lay them flat, and then cut those medallions into quarter circles. If you're using a globe eggplant, cut it into medallions, then into sixths, by halving and then cutting each half into three wedges. In a bowl, toss the eggplant pieces with the flour and cornstarch until evenly coated.

continued

Line a large plate with paper towels. In a sauté pan, heat the oil over high heat. Tilt the pan gently to see if the oil shimmers and makes streaks; if so, it's ready to use. Lower the heat to medium and add in half the eggplant, making sure the pieces don't over-lap. Let the eggplant fry undisturbed for 2 minutes. With a pair of tongs, carefully loosen the eggplant and turn to coat all sides with the oil. Fry for another 2 to 3 minutes, until the eggplant is crispy and golden brown. Some pieces might require more time in the pan than others. Transfer to the paper towel–lined plate and sprinkle with salt. Repeat this step with the remaining eggplant, adding a little more oil to the pan if it looks dry.

Once the eggplant is done, add the pasta to the boiling water and cook for 3 to 4 minutes, until tender but with a bit of bite. Drain the pasta and place it in a large bowl. With a pair of cook-ing chopsticks or a spoon, vigorously stir the pasta while slowly adding in the egg mixture. Divide the pasta among four serving bowls, then top each with a handful of crispy eggplant, a sprinkle of cheese, some black pepper, and flower petals or blossoms, if desired.

JALAPEÑO SHRIMP WITH CHARD + GRITS

When I first made this dish for others, it was March 6, the day of my sixteenth birthday. I was making the staff meal (aka family meal) for around fifty amazing team members at Gwen Butcher Shop & Restaurant, a restaurant in L.A., owned by Michelin-starred chef Curtis Stone. Chef Curtis is someone I think of as one of my first mentors. He was the host of *Top Chef Junior*, and his suggestions on camera always felt supportive while challenging me to be better. Off camera, he is very generous with his time. This dish is so special to me because it was one of the last chances I had to cook for a large group before the COVID-19 shelter-in-place quarantine restrictions took effect.

"Family meal" can mean a variety of things at a restaurant. Sometimes it is a challenge to an intern to create something delicious for the entire restaurant team. When my turn came to make family meal at Gwen, I was at once super excited and super terrified of cooking for them. I wanted to do something hardy yet light. Of course, it was L.A., so I wanted to include veggies and fruits. I made this shrimp-and-grits dish and served it with a salad similar to the Quick Green Zesty Salad on page 79, but with fried sunchokes, and a peachy version of the Strawberry Chamomile Pear Aguas (page 184) to drink. The team cleaned their plates completely!

As a side note, if you like more of a spicy kick, keep the seeds in the jalapeños. I almost always prefer stone-ground grits, where the germ and whole kernel are preserved, over quick or instant grits. The nutritional content is higher, and the taste is better.

SERVES 4

Grits
⅔ cup stone-ground grits, preferably organic

⅓ cup 2% milk

2 tablespoons unsalted butter

Kosher salt

Shrimp
½ yellow onion

3 garlic cloves

2 jalapeños, seeded

¼ cup plus 2 tablespoons extra-virgin olive oil

1 pound jumbo shrimp, peeled and deveined (see Cook's Note)

Chard
1 tablespoon extra-virgin olive oil

1 garlic clove, minced

1 bunch Swiss chard, stemmed and cut crosswise into 1-inch strips

Kosher salt

Herby Infused Oil (page 203) for serving

continued

Make the grits: In a stockpot or large cast-iron pot, combine the grits and 6 cups of water and bring to a boil over high heat. Decrease the heat to medium or medium-low (whichever keeps a light simmer and not a boil) and let cook for 1 hour. The grits will likely bubble, so don't forget to stir them occasionally and scrape the bottom of the pot with a wooden spoon so it doesn't scorch.

Meanwhile, marinate the shrimp: In a blender, combine the onion, garlic, jalapeños, and ¼ cup of the olive oil and process until smooth. Pour the sauce into a medium bowl, add the shrimp, and stir to coat. Refrigerate until it is time to cook the shrimp.

Make the chard: Heat a skillet over low heat and add the oil, garlic, and chard leaves and season with salt. Cook, stirring, until the chard begins to wilt, about 2 minutes. Cover the skillet with a lid and remove from the heat, which will allow the chard to continue wilting.

Once the grits have been cooking for 1 hour, add the milk and butter and season with salt. Stir, cover the pot, and let sit off the heat for 10 minutes.

Now, finish the shrimp: Place a large cast-iron skillet over medium heat and add the remaining 2 tablespoons of olive oil. Remove the bowl of shrimp from the fridge. Once the skillet is heated, lift each shrimp with tongs, let some sauce drip back into the bowl, and place into the skillet. Cook for about 2 minutes on each side, until pink and just starting to curl. You may need to brown the shrimp in two batches, depending on the size of your skillet. To serve, divide the grits among four shallow serving bowls, add small piles of chard to each, and top with the shrimp and Herby Infused Oil.

Cook's Note: You can leave the shrimp tails on or take them off here; the tails likely won't add much flavor. If you remove the shrimp tails, save or freeze them for when you make a stock.

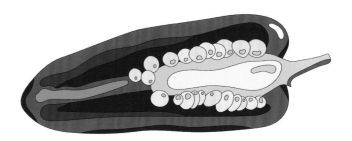

CORNFLOUR PANFRIED FISH

Panfrying is a technique where you use a small amount of oil to make something crispy. It is so crucial to a multitude of recipes across the Black diaspora: tostones, a crispy fried plantain; escoveitch, a whole panfried fish; corn cakes; to name a few. Here, panfrying allows the fish to get crispy while almost steaming out any extra water from the fish. This steam that escapes prevents the fish from leaching out steam after frying and making the coating soggy. Traditionally, panfrying is used to conserve oil while still producing a great result.

I grew up mostly vegetarian and with this recipe, we used tofu instead of fish. My three sisters and I were always encouraged to try whatever foods we wanted. I even developed a recipe for a day-in-the-life video for *Teen Vogue* in which I coated and panfried cabbage steaks and served them with the braised collards on page 83. So you can sub the fish in this recipe for something like tofu or cabbage. Really, this corn crust and panfrying technique has many applications. If you wanted to use tofu or a vegetable but keep it vegan, you could water down vegan mayo with a bit of nut milk as a substitute for the egg-milk mixture. I highly recommend eating this with a dash of hot sauce, which gives it an acidic and spicy bite.

SERVES 4 TO 6

1 cup corn flour (page 212) or store-bought (coarse-ground)

½ cup all-purpose flour

2 tablespoons creole seasoning (page 209)

Kosher salt

1 egg

1 cup 2% milk

Avocado oil or other neutral cooking oil for frying

4 to 6 tilapia fillets (about 2 pounds)

Hot sauce for serving (optional)

In a shallow dish that will accommodate the length of the tilapia fillets, whisk together the corn flour, all-purpose flour, creole sea-soning, and 2 teaspoons of salt. In a separate shallow dish, whisk together the egg and milk until thoroughly combined. Set both to the side. In a skillet that's at least 8 inches wide, pour enough oil to just coat the bottom of the pan, 2 to 4 tablespoons. Set over medium heat. Line a serving plate with paper towels.

continued

Coat one or two fillets at a time by dipping the tilapia in the milk-egg mixture, allowing any excess to drip off. Then place the fillet into the seasoned flour mixture and coat evenly on both sides. You can use a fork or tongs to move the fish from the wet to dry mixtures and use the fork to coat the fish without having to disturb or flip the fish too much. Working in batches so as not to crowd the pan, fry the fillets until browned on one side, about 2 minutes. Flip with a spatula and let the other side cook for about 2 minutes, until browned. Transfer the cooked fish to the paper towel–lined plate to drain, and repeat with the remaining fillets. If the pan starts to look dry, add a little more oil and allow it to heat up before adding more fish. Season with salt after removing from the pan. Spice with a few dashes of hot sauce (if you like some heat) and enjoy.

DAKGANGJEONG (KOREAN FRIED CHICKEN) + CHARD CABBAGE SLAW

Dakgangjeong is more commonly known in the United States as "KFC," or Korean fried chicken, and this recipe uses a sweet and sticky browned butter sauce. I panfry the thighs once, let the chicken drain, and then place the chicken in oil for a second time. Double frying allows the chicken to get super crispy and less oily. Dakgangjeong originated from the Black heritage culinary tradition. The Korean expression of fried chicken was thought to come from the dishes brought by the American military during the late 1940s. Fried chicken is often associated with deep-frying. But in Toni Tipton-Martin's cookbooks *Jubilee* and *The Jemima Code*, she writes that panfrying was the tradition, and that deep-frying was actually a result of fast-food commercialization of fried chicken. Panfrying is beneficial as it uses less oil and gives the chicken "air" to let out any water trapped when frying. It removes the water left from outside the chicken, making a crispier crust.

SERVES 4

Chicken

4 boneless, skinless chicken thighs, patted dry

3 teaspoons fine sea salt

1 egg

1 cup 2% milk

2 cups all-purpose flour

1 tablespoon chopped fresh rosemary leaves (from about 2 sprigs)

1 teaspoon chopped fresh thyme leaves (from about 1 sprig)

1 tablespoon grated lemon zest

2 cups neutral cooking oil

Slaw

½ of a 1-pound green cabbage, thinly sliced

½ bunch Swiss chard, stemmed and thinly sliced

2 tablespoons extra-virgin olive oil

2 tablespoons apple cider vinegar

2 tablespoons honey

1 garlic clove, minced

¼ teaspoon fine sea salt

¼ teaspoon freshly ground black pepper

Sauce

5 tablespoons unsalted butter

2 garlic cloves, crushed

3 tablespoons tamari

2 tablespoons honey

¼ cup natural cane sugar

continued

Season the chicken: With a small knife or kitchen scissors, cut off any excess fat from the thighs. Place a wire rack on a baking sheet, then place the chicken on the rack. Season both sides of the chicken thighs with 2 teaspoons of the salt and transfer to the fridge for 30 minutes. Prepare a clean cooling rack and baking sheet for when the chicken comes out of the oil later.

Meanwhile, make the slaw: In a large bowl, combine the cabbage and chard, then add the olive oil, apple cider vinegar, honey, and garlic. Mix thoroughly with salad tongs, then sprinkle with the salt and pepper. Set the bowl in the fridge for later.

Make the sauce: In a small saucepan over medium heat, combine the butter and garlic. Once the garlic browns, about 3 minutes, add the tamari, honey, and sugar. Cook, stirring constantly, for 2 minutes, or until the sauce bubbles and froths. Remove from the heat and let cool.

Set up your dredging station for the chicken: In a shallow dish, whisk together the egg and milk. In a second dish, mix together the flour, rosemary, thyme, lemon zest, and the remaining 1 teaspoon of salt. In a large cast-iron skillet, heat the vegetable oil over medium-high heat until it reads between 350° and 370°F on an instant-read thermometer. Set out a clean plate and cooling rack.

Coat the chicken: Dip a piece of chicken in the egg-milk mixture, let the excess drip off, then coat thoroughly in the flour mixture. Dip the same chicken thigh in egg and flour again, then place on the clean plate. Repeat with the remaining chicken thighs. Discard any leftover dredging mixtures.

Working in batches so as not to crowd the pan, fry the chicken for 4 minutes, flipping halfway through. Transfer the pieces to the clean cooling rack over a baking sheet while you fry the remaining thighs. Once all the thighs have been fried once, repeat the process, frying each thigh again for 4 minutes (flipping halfway), until the internal temperature is at least 165°F. When the chicken is done, let the pieces drain on the cooling rack, then toss them in the honey-brown butter sauce to coat. Return the pieces to the cooling rack to rest for 5 minutes. Serve with the slaw and enjoy!

WHOLE ROASTED LEMON PEPPER CHICKEN

This recipe is based on the mouthwatering flavor of lemon pepper in Black culinary traditions. There are different ways lemon pepper is used for seasoning. In the past, it was lemon pepper steaks, and we can credit Atlanta, Georgia, for the popularization of lemon pepper wings—a special mix of zesty, tart, spicy, and crispy wings. While lemon pepper steak may have fallen out of favor, the ever-present lemon pepper wings seem to never go out of style. But is such a demand sustainable? I wanted to do a whole-chicken recipe to show how easy it could be. If you prefer a vegan option, you can substitute a block of firm tofu cut into eight pieces with the flavors of this recipe, too. Brush the tofu with a small amount of oil, season, and roast on a baking sheet. Spatchcocking is used in this recipe for a wide range of reasons. Spatchcocking (cutting the backbone out of the chicken and gently pressing down on the breastbone to flatten) helps the chicken cook faster and more evenly. It also helps render the fat and keep the skin crispy.

SERVES 4 TO 6

3 lemons, zested

3 garlic cloves, grated on a Microplane grater

4 teaspoons fine sea salt

2 teaspoons freshly ground black pepper

1 whole chicken (4 to 4½ pounds), spatchcocked (see Cook's Note)

In a small bowl, combine the lemon zest, garlic, salt, and pepper, and set aside. Cut one of the zested lemons in half and reserve the extra lemons for different use.

In a large bowl, place the chicken and squeeze the juice of the cut lemon all over it. (To do this, you can place a fork into the flesh of the lemon, squeeze, and turn the fork to release the juice.) Pour the liquid that collects in the bottom of the bowl into the sink and place the bowl back on the counter. (If needed, wipe the outside of the bowl prior to placing it on the counter.) Using your hands, rub the lemon zest mixture all over the chicken. Let the chicken brine in the fridge for 1 hour.

continued

Preheat the oven to 250°F. Place a piece of aluminum foil or parchment paper into a roasting pan, then set a wire rack over the foil. Remove the chicken from the fridge to bring to room temperature for 30 minutes before roasting and place it breast-side up on the rack. Make sure the thighs and legs are turned out on either side of the chicken and not placed underneath.

Transfer the chicken to the oven for 20 minutes. When the time is up, rotate the pan 180 degrees and turn the oven up to 375°F. Roast the chicken for 20 minutes more. When this time is up, rotate the chicken 180 degrees again and cook for a final 20 minutes, or until an instant-read thermometer inserted into the thigh reads 165°F. If you don't have a thermometer, probe the thigh with a paring knife—if the juices run clear, it's ready. Remove the chicken from the oven and let it rest for about 10 minutes before carving and serving.

Cook's Note: You can ask your butcher to butterfly or "spatchcock" your chicken for you, or you can do it yourself: Place the chicken on a cutting board and discard the innards. Inspect the chicken: Sometimes a chicken may have tiny "hairs," which are actually the connective tissue from the feathers. There are all sorts of methods to get rid of them, but I recommend rubbing them with a paper towel or removing them with kitchen tweezers. Hold the chicken upright, almost like it's sitting up, and find the neck bone. With your knife, make a deep cut to the right side of the neck and down the right side of the back bone. Cut along the left side of the neck and backbone to remove it. If your knife struggles to cut through, make sure it's not hitting any bone near the thigh. Once the backbone is removed, with a knife or your hands, remove any fat or cartilage inside the cavity. Place the chicken breast-side up and press down on it with your hands until you can hear the ribs crack and the chicken lays as flat as possible.

RIBEYE TOSTADA WITH SQUASH MEDALLIONS + CREAMY BEANS

The region my family comes from in Mexico is called the Bajío, and it is home to the states Guanajuato, Jalisco, Aguascalientes, and Querétaro. It is known for different beef cooking techniques like asada, barbacoa, guisar, sofrier, and molar. In this recipe, I wanted to highlight world-renowned, delicious agriculture from Mexico like squash, beans, beef, and fresh herbs. I like this recipe because it contains a nice balanced bite of umami from the beans and beef, sweetness from the squash, and a slightly bitter and tart flavor from the herb salad. This dish first appeared on *Guy's Grocery Games*, and it won the hearts of judges. Luckily, I won the episode, and it is a recipe that people always ask me to share with them.

SERVES 4

3 tablespoons neutral cooking oil, such as avocado or grapeseed

1 (10-ounce) boneless ribeye steak

½ teaspoon fine sea salt

¼ teaspoon freshly ground black pepper

¼ cup unsalted butter

2 garlic cloves, crushed

1 (3-inch) sprig rosemary

1 yellow squash, sliced into ¼-inch-thick circles

1 cup creamy refried beans (page 96)

4 tostadas

½ cup fresh cilantro leaves

½ cup fresh dill leaves

2 tablespoons lime juice

1 avocado (optional)

In a cast-iron skillet, heat 2 tablespoons of the oil over medium heat for 2 minutes, or until the oil makes streaks in the skillet when tilted. Dry off the steak with paper towels and season both sides with salt and pepper.

Sear the steak for 3 minutes, then add the butter, garlic, and rosemary. Baste the steak for 3½ minutes by using a spoon and gently tilting the pan to lightly scoop the butter over the steak, until it changes to an even brownish color. Flip the steak and cook the other side, continuing to baste, for 4 more minutes. Transfer the steak to a cooling rack to rest for 5 minutes.

continued

While the steak is resting, wipe the pan clean. Heat the pan over medium heat and add the remaining 1 tablespoon of oil. After a minute or so, add the squash and cook for 2 minutes, flipping halfway through, until golden brown on each side.

Cut the steak against the grain into twelve slices. Spread ¼ cup of refried beans onto each tostada, then divide the squash evenly among the tostadas, arranging the slices in a circular pattern. Put three strips of steak on each tostada.

In a small bowl, combine the cilantro, dill, and lime juice and season with salt. Top each tostada with the herb salad. If you love avocado as much as I do, add sliced avocado on top of the steak, then add the herb salad.

PICNIC MENU INSPIRATION

Yachaejeon (Vegetable Pancakes) with Cho Ganjang (page 115)
+
Sweet + Salty Nori Popcorn (page 60)
+
Fruit Plate with Rose Scented Honey (page 30)
+
Glazed Pecans with Chocolate Drizzle + Bits (page 155)
+
Tie-Dye Berry Paletas (page 157)
+
Sun Chai (page 190)

Desserts —— 5

Desserts hold a special place in my culinary heart. As a five-year-old, desserts were one of my favorite things to cook. I would help pour flour and crack eggs into cake batter (and get an uncomfortable number of shells into the bowl). My oldest sister, Gabriella, made the best key lime pie and pecan pie. Even though I hated key lime pie at the time, cooking pies with Gabriella was more fun than any toy that I had. The first food I made by myself, at eight years old, was peach cream puffs. I loved cream puffs growing up, and when you're eight years old they aren't the most accessible to get. I was on a mission to make them myself and they turned out light, airy, and delicious.

The techniques in this chapter vary, from tempering to infusing to many others. Infusing is highlighted making Earl Grey glaze, oolong flan, and even paletas. I'm here to break a long-held myth that tempering chocolate is difficult. The Glazed Pecans with Chocolate Drizzle and Bits recipe (page 155) will make you never afraid to temper chocolate again. Tempering chocolate can seem complicated, but it's all about watching the numbers and letting it cool. The Glazed Pecans with Chocolate is a great recipe to try tempering for the first time.

MASA DOUGHNUTS WITH EARL GREY GLAZE

Masa is one of the great scientific and mathematical gifts of ancient Mexico. The act of processing dried corn kernels and creating a chemical lime solution to make something so versatile from corn, amazes me endlessly. This masa dough gives another level of flavor complexity and subtle sweetness to the classic glazed doughnut. I first started working on this recipe on the same day that I was getting interviewed by cookbook author Julia Turshen for *Food & Wine*. I was a big fan of Julia's before we met and she has been a great supporter of mine and countless others. When the interview was over, we started chatting about things we'd made recently and I talked about these doughnuts. Her response was an enthusiastic "yum!" and just hearing that response was so encouraging to me. Sometimes, just a small word of cheer goes a long way.

You can save the leftover frying oil for another frying project. It should not need to be strained because these doughnuts hold together during the frying process. To store, keep in a dark, cool area with an airtight lid for 1 month, or until it starts to smell off.

MAKES 4 DOUGHNUTS

Doughnuts
⅔ cup whole milk

¼ cup unsalted butter

2¼ teaspoons (¼-ounce envelope) active dry yeast

2¼ cups all-purpose flour

½ cup masa harina

¼ cup natural cane sugar

½ teaspoon fine sea salt

1 egg

2 quarts neutral cooking oil

Glaze
½ cup whole milk

2 teaspoons loose-leaf Earl Grey tea (or 2 tea bags)

1 teaspoon vanilla extract

2¼ cups confectioners' sugar

To make the doughnuts: In a saucepan, combine the milk and butter and heat until lukewarm (90°F). Don't worry about the butter melting all the way yet. Transfer to a small bowl, add the yeast, gently stir, and let sit for 5 minutes, until foamy.

In the bowl of a stand mixer or in a large bowl, combine the flour, masa, cane sugar, and salt. Mix at the lowest speed or by hand until

continued

combined. Slowly add the milk-yeast mixture and mix, but not thoroughly. Beat the egg in a small bowl, then slowly add it to the dough, and mix again until combined. Scrape down the sides of the bowl, then continue mixing on medium speed until the dough just comes together but isn't smooth yet, about 4 minutes. Place the dough onto an oiled cutting board and knead for 3 to 5 minutes, until smooth.

Lightly oil a mixing bowl and place the dough in it. Cover the bowl with plastic wrap or a damp kitchen towel, and let the dough rise in a warm place for 1 to 1½ hours, until roughly doubled in size. Dust a cutting board with flour and pour out the dough. Roll out the dough with a rolling pin until it's ½ inch thick. Using a 3- or 4-inch ring mold, cut out four circles. Using a small 1-inch ring mold, cut out doughnut holes from the circles and the remaining dough. If you don't have ring molds, a large-mouthed glass jar and a piping tip will do just fine. You could even roll out the excess dough into a rope and cut 1-inch pieces to make more holes. Either way, space the doughnuts out on a baking sheet, cover, and let rise for 30 minutes.

While your dough is doing its final rise, make the glaze. In a small saucepan over medium-low heat, add the milk and Earl Grey tea. (If you're using tea bags, cut them open and empty out the leaves into the milk.) As soon as the milk comes to a simmer, cover the pan and take it off the heat. Let infuse for 20 minutes. Add the vanilla. Place the confectioners' sugar in a medium bowl and place a fine-mesh sieve on top. Pour the milk mixture through the sieve into the confectioners' sugar. Whisk until completely combined and set aside.

Place a cooling rack on top of a baking sheet (or just set out a baking sheet). Fill a large saucepan with the oil and heat on medium-high until it reaches 315°F on an instant-read thermometer. Working in batches, fry the doughnuts for 3 minutes on each side and the holes for 1 minute on each side, turning with a slotted metal spoon, until golden brown. Don't crowd the pot and keep an eye on the temperature, adjusting the heat as needed to maintain 315°F.

When the doughnuts are done, place them on the cooling rack (or baking sheet). Let cool slightly. Spoon some glaze over each doughnut and hole and serve. I find these doughnuts are best the same day they're cooked. But they will last until the next day, especially if warmed.

OOLONG TEA FLAN WITH BROWN SUGAR CARAMEL

Flan traditionally has a custardy base with a thin but rich caramel on top, and this recipe is no different. One of my favorite parts of this recipe is the steaming technique. Steaming the flan was inspired by the Chinese method of steaming savory egg custard. Normally, flan would go into a water bath in a hot oven for around an hour. But a water bath can end with hot water splashing onto your hands as you stressfully try to maneuver the flan out of the oven. In this recipe, the flan steams on the stove top for only fifteen minutes, taking down the cooking time drastically. Another difference is the brown sugar, which caramelizes faster and at a lower temperature than natural cane or granulated sugar. Oolong tea is a slightly fermented Chinese tea that falls in between green and black. Make sure you're buying a darker oolong, as one labeled as green oolong will have too light a flavor. The oolong from Yamamotoyama works and is easy to find at Asian grocery stores or online.

SERVES 6

Flan

2 cups 2% milk, plus more as needed

1 tablespoon oolong tea leaves (from about 3 emptied tea bags)

1 (14-ounce) can sweetened condensed milk, preferably organic

3 eggs

3 egg yolks

½ teaspoon fine sea salt

Brown Sugar Caramel

½ cup firmly packed dark brown sugar

1 tablespoon corn syrup, preferably organic

To make the flan, start by making evaporated milk. In a saucepan, combine the milk and oolong tea leaves. Heat over medium heat for 20 minutes, stirring periodically to prevent a skin from forming and to prevent the bottom from scorching. Let the milk cool down in the freezer if you want to make the dessert quickly, or the fridge if you want to break up the steps.

Meanwhile, in a large bowl, whisk together the condensed milk, eggs, egg yolks, and salt. Strain this mixture into a medium bowl.

continued

Once the evaporated milk is cold (about 25 minutes in the freezer and 45 minutes to 1 hour in the fridge), strain it into a measuring cup. You should get 1 cup of infused milk. (It's okay if a few specks of tea make their way into the milk.) If you have less, top it off with a little more milk so you get to 1 cup. Add the milk to the egg mixture and whisk together.

Set six ramekins out on a countertop and start on the brown sugar caramel. In a saucepan over medium-high heat, combine 2 tablespoons of water with the brown sugar and corn syrup. Monitoring with an instant-read thermometer, heat the caramel to 250°F. It should take 3 to 4 minutes. Once the temperature hits 250°F, take the pan off the heat and swirl in 2 more tablespoons of water. Evenly distribute the brown sugar caramel among the ramekins, spooning about 1 tablespoon into each.

Evenly divide the egg mixture into the ramekins by pouring about ½ cup into each ramekin. Cover the ramekins tightly with aluminum foil or plastic wrap.

In a large pot fitted with a steamer insert, bring 1 cup of water to a boil over high heat. If you do not have a steamer, form a few sheets of aluminum foil into 1-inch-thick nest-like shapes each, large enough to hold a ramekin and sit securely while being steamed. You want the foil to be just slightly above the water. Once the water is boiling, lower the heat to medium to maintain a simmer. With tongs, gently place three ramekins into the steamer or on the squares of foil, ensuring they don't touch the water, and steam, covered, for 15 minutes. The flans should look mostly set, with a slight wobble in the center. (They'll finish cooking as they cool.) If they still look liquidy, re-cover the flans and steam for 2 more minutes. Cook the next batch of three ramekins the same way, adding more water to the pot if necessary.

Let the flans cool to room temperature. Run a butter knife around the inside edges of the ramekins to release the flans, then flip each one upside down onto a plate. You could flip them out while they're still warm, but if you wait until they cool, they'll have a firmer texture and better flavor. Serve immediately or store in the fridge tightly covered with foil or plastic wrap for 4 to 5 days.

GLAZED PECANS WITH CHOCOLATE DRIZZLE + BITS

The rich, toasty, and buttery pecan-and-chocolate flavor balance great with the dash of lemon juice for these glazed pecans. I like to pay attention to the cacao percentages when eating chocolate and when experimenting with chocolate for baking. The percentage is based on the cocoa mass divided by the total weight of the bar. A higher number often means more cocoa, less sugar, and fewer fillers. The dark chocolate I use in this recipe is 75% cacao, but anything you find in the baking aisle in the 70 to 75% range will work. Tempering chocolate can be intimidating, but I believe this dependable tempering technique will ease any potential failures. Some people claim you can temper chocolate without using an instant read thermometer, but I don't recommend that approach. The instant read thermometer helps your accuracy, and thermometer-free "hacks" do not give consistent results. There are a variety of thermometers that have a lifetime guarantee and are not super expensive. It is important to be mindful about your kitchen's temperature and level of humidity, as a higher kitchen temperature might result in a longer cooling time for your chocolate.

SERVES 4 TO 6

1 tablespoon unsalted butter

2 cups unsalted pecan halves, toasted

⅓ cup firmly packed dark brown sugar

2 teaspoons lemon juice

7 ounces bittersweet chocolate (70 to 75% cacao), chopped

1 teaspoon flaky sea salt

Line a baking sheet with parchment paper or a silicone mat and set aside. In a skillet, melt the butter on medium heat. Add the pecans and toast for 3 minutes, stirring constantly, until they smell toasty (they should not brown much). Add the brown sugar and lemon juice and turn the heat down to low. Allow the sugar to melt for 2 to 4 minutes, stirring constantly, until you can see the liquid sugar pool at the bottom. Spread the pecans out onto the prepared baking sheet and set aside.

continued

To temper the chocolate, use a stainless-steel double boiler, or a heatproof bowl that fits securely on top of a saucepan also works. Add a couple inches of water to the saucepan and bring it to a boil. When you place the double-boiler insert or bowl on top, make sure the bottom doesn't touch the water. Add 3 ounces of the chocolate to the insert or bowl and melt it to 90°F, stirring occasionally with a heatproof spatula. If you accidentally let the temperature rise higher than 90°F, don't worry. Just don't let the chocolate pass 120°F because it will burn. Remove the insert or bowl from the pan of water and set it on a kitchen towel on a counter.

Add the remaining 4 ounces of chocolate to the saucepan, stirring occasionally, until the temperature reaches 84°F on an instant-read thermometer. This will take about 15 minutes.

Place the insert or bowl back over the water and start boiling the water again. Let the temperature of the chocolate come up to 87°F. This should take only about 30 seconds so keep a close eye on it.

With a fork, drizzle the chocolate over the pecans until you're satisfied with the look of them, then allow the chocolate to harden. Get a clean piece of parchment paper and spread out the leftover chocolate into a thin layer on top of it. Sprinkle with the salt and allow the chocolate to harden, 15 to 25 minutes. Once the chocolate has hardened, break it up into small pieces with your hands and place it in a serving bowl with the pecans. Store, sealed, at room temperature, for 2 to 3 weeks.

TIE-DYE BERRY PALETAS

I've heard paletas described as Mexican popsicles. This always seemed so wrong because the name *paletas* literally means "little shovel," and their mind-boggling flavor varieties—some bordering on savory—never seemed comparable to popsicles, besides them both being frozen. Paletas can come in a wide variety of flavors, from coconut to tamarind, can include milk, and sometimes a thickening agent, like agar or gelatin. Most commonly, paletas are fruit-flavored with some kind of fruit or pulp inside. This recipe combines three different fruit flavors: blackberries, strawberries, and blueberries. It's a great recipe for younger cooks as well. My five-year-old brother, Land, and I make it together. I find that blending, minimal cutting, boiling, and freezing are really great introductory skills to learn. This recipe makes a little bit of extra liquid which an average-size popsicle mold might not be able to fit. I recommend stirring any leftover paleta syrup into mineral water for a bubbly and refreshing drink.

MAKES 6 TO 8 PALETAS

1 pound strawberries, hulled

¼ cup plus 2 tablespoons natural cane sugar

Zest of 1 lime

¾ cup (about 6 ounces) blueberries

¾ cup (about 6 ounces) blackberries

2 teaspoons lime juice

In a blender, combine the strawberries, ¼ cup of the sugar, and 1 cup of water. Blend until the strawberries turn into a smooth liquid. Transfer the mixture to a saucepan and bring it to a simmer over medium heat. Continue to cook for 5 minutes until it looks slightly thickened and the color intensifies. Strain the strawberry mixture through a fine-mesh sieve into a bowl. What's left in the sieve will be mostly seeds and can be composted. Stir the lime zest into the strawberry mixture and set it to the side to infuse.

While the strawberries are infusing, start on your other berry mixture. In the same blender (no need to rinse it out), blend the blueberries, blackberries, the remaining ½ cup of water, and the remaining 2 tablespoons of sugar. In the same pan (no need to rinse it out) over medium heat, bring the blueberry-blackberry

continued

mixture to a simmer, then cook for 5 minutes, until the berries start to thicken. Strain through a fine-mesh sieve into a separate bowl. What's left in the sieve can be composted. Stir the lime juice into the blueberry mixture.

Get out your popsicle molds. I find that most molds fit about ½ cup of liquid. Pour ⅓ cup of the strawberry mixture into each popsicle mold. Then, slowly pour or spoon 2 tablespoons of the blueberry-blackberry mixture into each mold. Insert popsicle sticks and freeze overnight.

When the paletas are frozen and you're ready to eat, run the molds under warm water to help release the paletas. Store leftovers in the freezer for up to a month.

CITRUS SALAD WITH HIBISCUS SYRUP + LIME SALT

Fruit vendors are such a staple of my food memories. Year-round in Oakland, California it's common to find small vendor carts filled with fruits such as mango, cucumber, and papaya and toppings like Tajín, chamoy, and lime juice. I've loved sharing a quart of fresh mango and cucumber with my sisters after a long walk. Once the fruit was gone, a tart and tangy mixture of lime, mango juice, Tajín, and chamoy would sit at the bottom until my sister Fidela would drink the entire thing. This recipe is reminiscent of the best parts of growing up in Oakland, plus the leftover fruit liquid and one of my all-time favorite flavors, hibiscus.

SERVES 4

¼ cup dried hibiscus

¼ cup natural cane sugar

1 medium navel orange

1 blood orange

1 grapefruit

Zest of 1 small lime

2 teaspoons flaky sea salt

In a small saucepan, combine the hibiscus, ¼ cup of water, and the sugar and bring to a gentle simmer over medium-high heat. Stir to dissolve the sugar and allow the syrup to cook down until it has slightly thickened and is lightly bubbling, about 7 minutes. Carefully strain the syrup into a heatproof cup or bowl and let sit in the fridge for 15 minutes.

While the syrup is cooling down, start on the fruit. Cut the tops and bottoms off the oranges and grapefruit, then use the knife to slowly cut the peel down from around the fruit. For this step, use the top of the fruit as a visual guide to cut the peel away from the flesh. Once the oranges and grapefruit are removed from their peels, place them on their sides and cut them into ½-inch-thick medallions.

Arrange the fruit on a big plate and set to the side. Mix the lime zest with the flaky salt in a small bowl. With a fork, drizzle half of the cooled hibiscus syrup over the fruit. Then sprinkle half the lime salt over the fruit. Serve with the rest of the hibiscus and lime salt on the side in case you want more.

BLACKBERRY LEMON TRES LECHES CAKE

Tres leches is often served as a birthday cake, but in a lot of local panaderías, or Mexican bakeries, it can be sold by the slice. Baking the cake in a pie plate creates a wonderful shape and less mess than making a layered cake, because the milks used are contained in the pie pan. This tres leches cake combines the creaminess of tres leches cake with the sweet and tart flavor of berries. Berries and cream are always a good pair. Blackberries work great, but if not available, I recommend using raspberries, strawberries, or your favorite soft, sweet, and sour fruit. I believe it's the understated sweetness from the cake, berries, and whipped cream that make this dessert special.

SERVES 6 TO 8

¼ cup unsalted butter, at room temperature

¾ cup natural cane sugar

¼ cup neutral cooking oil

2 eggs

1½ cups all-purpose flour

¼ teaspoon fine sea salt

1½ teaspoons baking powder

⅔ cup whole milk

½ cup sweetened condensed milk, preferably organic

1 (12-ounce) can evaporated milk, preferably organic

¾ cup (about 6 ounces) blackberries

1 cup heavy cream

2 tablespoons confectioners' sugar

Zest from 1 lemon

Preheat the oven to 350°F. Butter a 9-inch metal pie pan or 9-inch round cake pan. In a large bowl, cream together the butter and cane sugar by beating it with a wooden spoon. Once smooth, beat in the oil, then the eggs, one at a time.

In a separate bowl, combine the flour, salt, and baking powder. Gently stir about a fourth of the flour mixture into the creamed butter mixture, then about a fourth of the whole milk. Continue slowly incorporating the flour and milk in three more additions. It's okay if the batter is not totally smooth. Pour into the prepared cake pan and bake for 25 to 28 minutes, until a toothpick inserted in the center comes out clean. Let the cake cool in the fridge until at least room temperature (about 30 minutes).

continued

In a small bowl, combine the condensed milk and evaporated milk. When the cake has finished cooling, poke holes all over it with a wooden dowel or fork. Slowly pour the condensed milk mixture over the cake, pausing to allow the milks to seep into the cake. This can take several minutes. You should be able to use all of the milk mixture, but it's okay if you have a little left over.

Reserve 4 blackberries for a garnish. Place the rest of the blackberries into a small bowl and mash. Pour the blackberries and juice onto the cake in an even layer.

In a separate bowl, whip together the heavy cream and confectioners' sugar until you get soft peaks. Scoop the whipped cream on top of the cake. Slice the reserved blackberries in half lengthwise, then place them on top of the cake. Sprinkle with the lemon zest, if desired.

CHOCOLATE CHERRY CHEESECAKE COOKIES

These cookies are delicious on their own, but the cherry cheesecake topping creates a yummy contrast with the rich-but-not-overly-sweet chocolate. I recommend using your favorite brand of snacking chocolate for this recipe rather than a bar of baking chocolate. You can even experiment with different percentages of chocolate, like milk, white, semi-sweet, or in this case, dark. If you don't plan on serving all the cookies at once, I recommend placing the unfrosted cookies into a sealed container in the fridge and reheating in the oven until just warm and soft. If you want to save the whipped topping, it can be refrigerated in a sealed container for no more than a week.

MAKES 5 OR 6 LARGE COOKIES

6 tablespoons unsalted butter, cubed, at room temperature

½ cup firmly packed light brown sugar

1 egg

1 cup all-purpose flour

⅓ cup natural cocoa powder

½ teaspoon baking soda

4 ounces dark chocolate (70% cacao), chopped into ¼- to ½-inch chunks

Cherry Cheesecake Topping

3 ounces cream cheese, room temperature

½ cup heavy cream, cold

2 tablespoons confectioners' sugar

⅓ cup frozen pitted cherries

Squeeze of lemon

2 tablespoons light brown sugar

Preheat the oven to 350°F. Line a baking sheet with parchment paper and set aside.

In a large bowl, combine the butter and brown sugar. Cream the butter and sugar by smashing them together with a whisk until smooth and well combined, scraping the whisk with a rubber spatula as needed. Whisk in the egg.

In a small bowl, combine the flour, cocoa powder, and baking soda. Stir half of the flour mixture into the butter mixture with a rubber spatula until almost combined. Add the chocolate chunks, then add the remaining flour mixture.

continued

With a dry ⅓-cup measuring cup, portion out 5 or 6 cookies. Roll each cookie into a ball and press it flat on the cutting board to be about ½ inch thick. Place the cookies on the prepared baking sheet, about ½ inch apart. Bake for 10 minutes. The surface of the cookies should feel dry if you lightly touch them. Transfer the cookies to a cooling rack and allow them to cool for about 10 minutes.

While the cookies are cooling, prepare the cherry cheesecake topping. In a large bowl, use an electric mixer with a whisk attachment to whip the cream cheese, heavy cream, and confectioners' sugar until it resembles the stiffness of whipped cream. This will take several minutes, and it's okay if the mixture isn't totally smooth. When done, place the whipped topping into the fridge. Rinse the cherries (no need to defrost them) and coarsely chop them on a cutting board. Place the cherries into a small saucepan with the lemon juice and brown sugar. Let the cherries reduce over medium-high heat for about 4 minutes until the liquid is mostly gone and the cherries are sticky. Let cool.

To assemble, evenly divide the whipped topping among the cookies, and spread with a butter knife. Make a small indent in the middle of the whipped topping on each cookie by tilting a small spoon in a circular motion. Evenly divide the cherry compote among the cookies by placing a small amount in each indent. These are best eaten right away, but you can store leftovers in the fridge for up to a week.

CRUNCH CAKE BARS

This recipe is a great showcase for the kitchen technique of tempering. Tempering is a method combining at least two different ingredients at different temperatures that are brought to a similar temperature. If you have ever made a béchamel or an alfredo sauce, you have used the tempering method. It is used in savory and sweet cooking, from sauces to dishes involving eggs to chocolate and sugar work. In this recipe, tempering is about controlling the temperature of sugar to create a wide variety of textures and flavors, ranging from thick and rich to crunchy and light. Tempered sugar can become syrups for drinks, snappy and shiny chocolate, chewy caramel, and in this case, a light and airy crunchy candy called honeycomb or sea foam. This crunch cake bar is a soft sponge cake topped with whipped cream and crunched honeycomb, inspired by the crunch cake at Eastern Bakery, the oldest bakery in San Francisco's Chinatown. The one from Eastern Bakery has some unique elements beyond the sea-foam sugar and coffee flavor, and the cake is more of a Chinese cake style than German or Louisianan. The Chinese style of cake is fluffier, less dense, and not overly sweet. Another difference is that the sea-foam sugar is really reflective of the Chinese cooking technique of cutting foods into small pieces and not large chunks as found in the German or Louisianan versions. This perspective is important because it demonstrates Chinese food culture's authority in sugar work and pastry knowledge. Additionally, Chinese American restaurants in the US emerged at the beginning of American restaurant history. This cannot be said enough, as the erasure of this fact ignores the historic contributions Chinese Americans made toward the development of American restaurant industry.

MAKES 8 CAKE BARS

Cake

1 tablespoon unsalted butter for pan

3 egg yolks

¼ cup natural cane sugar

¼ cup vegetable oil

3 tablespoons whole milk

½ cup all-purpose flour

3 egg whites

¼ teaspoon cream of tartar

Coffee Whipped Topping

1 cup heavy cream

1 teaspoon instant coffee

3 tablespoons confectioners' sugar

Coffee Crunch

1 cup natural cane sugar

¼ cup strong cold brew coffee or espresso

¼ cup corn syrup

2 teaspoons baking soda

continued

For the cake: Line an 8-inch square baking pan with parchment paper and butter it. Set it to the side.

Place the yolks in a large bowl with 2 tablespoons of the cane sugar. Whisk until incorporated. Whisk in the oil and milk. Sift in the flour and whisk until smooth. Don't worry about overmixing, as this batter is forgiving. Set to the side.

Preheat the oven to 375°F. In a separate, clean and dry mixing bowl, beat the egg whites with an electric whisk or stand mixer with the whisk attachment. Beat on low until the eggs are frothy. Add the cream of tartar, then slowly increase the speed while pouring in the remaining 2 tablespoons of cane sugar. You want the egg whites to reach soft peaks, where the fluffy whites curve at the end of your whisk.

Fold a third of the whipped egg whites into the batter to help loosen the yolk mixture. The yolks can be a little stubborn, so fold until completely incorporated. Fold in the next third of egg whites, being more careful this time to gently incorporate and not deflate the egg whites. Add the last of the egg whites—again, carefully— and then pour into the prepared pan. Bake for 15 minutes, or until the top of the cake looks slightly brown. I don't recommend using a toothpick to check the cake, as this can make it deflate. If it springs back when touched lightly, it should be cooked. Clear a spot on your counter for the cake to go, right out of the oven. Immediately after removing the cake pan from the oven, drop it onto the counter from an inch high. (This might sound strange, but it helps the cake not deflate so much.) Let the cake cool on a cooling rack and start on the toppings.

For the coffee whipped topping: Stir together the heavy cream and instant coffee. Let sit in the fridge to dissolve while you start the coffee crunch.

For the coffee crunch: Line a baking sheet with parchment paper and set it to the side. Get out a whisk and an instant-read thermometer. In a large saucepan, combine the cane sugar, coffee, and corn syrup. Give this a stir with a rubber spatula and make sure to scrape around the inside of the pan. Set the pan over medium heat and, using your thermometer, wait for it to come to 300°F. Remove from the heat and immediately whisk in the baking soda until just combined. Quickly but gently pour the mixture onto the prepared baking sheet. Do not spread the mixture out or it will deflate. Let it cool completely.

While the candy crunch is cooling, whisk the coffee-infused heavy cream with the confectioners' sugar until it looks like softly whipped cream.

To assemble, remove the cake from its pan and trim the brown edges. Top the cake with a ½-inch layer of coffee whipped cream, making sure to cover the corners. With a large knife, cut the cake into 8 rectangular bars. Crush the coffee crunch into tiny pieces no more than ⅔ inch in size, and top the cake with your desired amount.

BROWN BUTTER BILLIONAIRE BARS

I wanted to create a dessert to celebrate Mansa Musa. He is one of the richest people, if not the richest person, ever to have lived. He ruled over a kingdom that spanned more than eight present-day countries, such as Mali, Burkina Faso, and Mauritania. Mansa Musa was known for his elaborate gift giving. Apparently he gave away so much gold that he affected the price of gold for some time. For me, he is the reminder that luxury and prosperity do not originate in American or European capitalism. He's also a great reminder that Black and brown people originate from a wealth of resources, and that our intellectual capacity and ingenuity are true wealth. This recipe name comes mainly from the browned butter and brown sugar that put this shortbread recipe over the top.

MAKES 8 BARS

Shortbread
¾ cup (1½ sticks) unsalted butter

¼ cup firmly packed dark brown sugar

¼ teaspoon fine sea salt

1½ cups all-purpose flour

2 tablespoons whole milk

Caramel
1½ cups natural cane sugar

3 tablespoons corn syrup

¼ teaspoon fine sea salt

7 tablespoons heavy cream

2 tablespoons unsalted butter

Chocolate
2 cups (12 ounces) semi-sweet chocolate baking chips

½ teaspoon flaky sea salt

Make the shortbread: Melt the butter over medium heat for about 10 minutes, until the butter slightly darkens and smells toasty. Cool the browned butter in the fridge until it's about room temperature, about 20 minutes.

Preheat the oven to 350°F. Line an 8-inch square baking pan with parchment paper, leaving about an inch of paper hanging over two sides. Butter the pan and set it to the side. (You can try to grease the pan with the butter wrapper to reduce waste.)

Once the butter is cooled, place it in a large mixing bowl and add the brown sugar and salt. Stir until fully combined. Slowly stir in the flour and milk. Place the dough into the prepared pan, patting it down into as even a layer as possible. That way, when you add the caramel on top, it looks neat and sets evenly. With a fork, poke holes into the shortbread crust to prevent it from puffing. Bake for 20 to 25 minutes, until the shortbread starts to brown around the edges. Take the shortbread out of the oven and let it cool on a potholder or kitchen towel in the fridge.

Make the caramel: While your shortbread is cooling, combine the cane sugar, ¼ cup of water, the corn syrup, and salt in a large, heavy saucepan. Cover and bring to a boil over medium-high heat, for 3 to 5 minutes, until the sugar has melted. Uncover and cook until the sugar looks pale gold in color and hits 300°F on an instant-read thermometer, 4 to 5 minutes. Turn the heat down to medium and cook for a few minutes more, until the sugar is deep gold and registers 350°F. Remove from the heat and add the cream in a slow stream. Add the butter and stir until evenly combined. Let the mixture cool for 5 minutes, then pour it onto the shortbread. Place the shortbread back into the fridge until the caramel cools to around room temperature, about 20 minutes.

For the chocolate: Use a stainless-steel double boiler, or a heat-proof bowl that fits securely on top of a saucepan works well, too. Add a couple inches of water to the pan and bring it to a boil. When you place the double-boiler insert or bowl on top, make sure the bottom doesn't touch the water. Place 1½ cups of the chocolate chips into the insert or bowl and stir with a rubber spatula until the chocolate reaches 115°F on an instant-read thermometer. Take the insert or bowl off the heat and add the remaining ½ cup of chocolate chips and sea salt. Stir in the chips and let sit until the temperature has come down to 84°F. (This can take as long as 20 minutes.)

Place the insert or bowl back onto the saucepan and start boiling the water again. Let the temperature reach 87°F. (This can be as fast as 30 seconds, so keep an eye on it.) Pour the chocolate onto the caramel and let it set up in the fridge, about 20 minutes. Use the parchment paper to remove the shortbread from the baking pan and cut into 8 bars. Serve or store in the fridge for up to 2 weeks.

AFTERNOON TEA MENU INSPIRATION

Citrus Salad with Hibiscus Syrup + Lime Salt (page 161)

+

Salmon Bagel Spread (page 35)

+

Concha Scones (page 49)

+

Strawberry Chamomile Pear Aguas (page 184)

+

Sun Chai (page 190)

6

Drinks

This drink chapter contains nonalcoholic beverages from all over the world, and it highlights how different cultures and ingredients combine together. The New Orleans-style Vietnamese Iced Coffee (page 194) uses the Vietnamese coffee-roasting technique and combines it with the unique Louisianan tradition of chicory-infused coffee with condensed milk. The Jamaica and Pineapple Punch (page 180) is another drink that crosses multiple cultures. Jamaica tea, which comes from hibiscus flower sepals, is drunk worldwide, from Mexico and Jamaica to Senegal, Thailand, Italy, and Haiti. This Jamaica and Pineapple punch recipe uses the entire pineapple: the juice to help sweeten the drink and the rind to infuse even more flavor into the Jamaica tea. Both recipes are wonderful cold drinks that are refreshing on a warm day.

The primary technique used in this chapter is infusing. Infusing is used in almost every drink. I love infusing drinks because it can be done at any temperature. With low heat, the Sun Chai (page 190) works great. Heat, like boiling, is used to infuse flavor from fruits and dried teas in recipes like the Sharab Rose Raspberry Shrub (page 183), Ginger Spritzer (page 179), and the Jamaica and Pineapple Punch. Recipes like Oat Horchata (page 193) or 8-Hour Cold Brew (page 195) work great if you want a cold, subtle infused flavor.

If you're looking for inspiration for a meal, the Strawberry Chamomile Pear Aguas (page 184) pair great with the Mole Verde Maitake Mushroom Tacos (page 122). The floral and fruity notes from the aguas work well with the earthy notes of the corn tortilla and maitake mushrooms. The Sun Chai is an excellent companion to the Miser Wot (page 117).

GINGER SPRITZER

I love eating at Jamaican restaurants that serve ginger beer, and I order it whenever I can get my hands on it. A cool glass always complements spiced and slow-cooked dishes like brown stew, callaloo, and jerk. Ginger beer is made from a multiday fermentation process that allows natural bubbles to form. When you want a version of ginger beer but might not have the time to ferment, this recipe is a great fix. This ginger spritzer has the flavors of ginger beer and uses sparkling mineral water to replace the fermentation process.

SERVES 4

2 thumb-size pieces unpeeled ginger, grated on a Microplane grater

⅓ cup still water

⅓ cup maple syrup

4 cups sparkling mineral water

1 tablespoon lime juice

In a saucepan, combine the ginger, still water, and maple syrup and cook on low for 15 minutes, until thicker in texture. Let the liquid cool in the fridge for about 45 minutes. The longer it steeps, the spicier and stronger it will become. When ready to serve, strain the mixture into a pitcher and add the sparkling water and lime juice. Serve in chilled glasses.

JAMAICA + PINEAPPLE PUNCH

I always think of this recipe as one for celebrations and dinner parties, and it is something that can be made ahead, as the flavors develop over time. Dried hibiscus has a variety of uses in different cultures, and I really marvel at the savory uses, like dried hibiscus carne asada. The use of pineapple peels and fresh pineapple add extra flavor and body to the drink, too! Make sure to strain well after blending the pineapple to avoid any grittiness. Don't bother to spend extra time slowly cutting off each eye on the pineapple, because they will end up getting blended and strained out.

SERVES 8

½ pineapple
1 cup dried hibiscus
8 cups distilled or spring water

½ cup natural cane sugar or agave nectar
1 tablespoon lime juice
Ice for serving

Rinse the pineapple and cut off the skin. Coarsely chop up the skin and measure out 1 cup (you can freeze the rest for future use). Cut out the core, cut it into pieces, and place the pieces in a medium saucepan with the pineapple skin. Coarsely chop the remaining pineapple flesh, measure out 2 heaping cups, and set aside. Eat the rest as a snack or freeze for future use.

Add the hibiscus and 2 cups of the water to the pan, then bring the mixture to a boil over high heat. Once boiling, decrease the heat to a low simmer for 5 minutes. Strain the mixture and allow it to cool. (You can place it in the freezer to speed up the cooling process.)

Put the 2 cups of pineapple flesh into a blender with the sugar and 4 cups of the water. Blend for 30 seconds until smooth and pale yellow, then strain the mixture into a large pitcher, discarding the solids.

Add the cooled hibiscus liquid to the pitcher along with the remaining 2 cups of water and the lime juice. Stir and serve in glasses with ice. This will keep in the fridge for 4 to 5 days.

SHARAB ROSE RASPBERRY SHRUB

This drink is inspired by the rose-flavored drink known as sharab el ward. While you can find sharab el ward in Lebanon, Syria, Palestine, and Jordan, this one is inspired by the Lebanese version. My recipe also nods to the tradition of the shrub, which is a vinegary, pungent drink that in seventeenth-century England was made with alcohol or a vinegar syrup. This version is the nonalcoholic vinegar syrup variety. Vinegar-based beverages infused with fruit and used for soft drinks or cocktails can be found globally. This pairing of fragrant rose, subtly floral raspberries, and tart vinegar works so well.

SERVES 4

⅓ cup natural cane sugar

⅓ cup distilled or spring water

1 cup (about 4 ounces) raspberries

⅓ cup distilled white vinegar

2 tablespoons rose water

Ice for serving

4 cups sparkling or still water

In a small saucepan, combine the sugar and water and bring to a simmer over high heat. Cook for 4 minutes, until syrupy. Place the raspberries in a bowl, mash with a fork, and add to the pan. Decrease the heat to medium-low and cook for 5 minutes, until the liquid mixture starts to thicken. Add the vinegar and rose water and cook for 3 minutes, until the rose-and-vinegar smell permeates the air. Strain the shrub into a heat-resistant glass jar and let cool in the fridge.

Add ice and 1 cup of sparkling or still water to four 12-ounce glasses. Pour the shrub evenly among the glasses and serve. The shrub will keep in the fridge for 3 to 4 days.

STRAWBERRY CHAMOMILE PEAR AGUAS

Agua fresca translates directly to "fresh water." Aguas come in many flavors, from chia-cucumber to strawberry to pineapple. They are a remnant from before Spanish colonization in Mexico, starting out as fruit-infused water with ice from dormant Mexican volcanoes. Nowadays, the fruit is often blended or juiced. Aguas frescas normally consist of fruit, water, and sometimes a sweetener of natural cane sugar or agave. This version is inspired by the aguas at the Michelin-starred restaurant Californios, in San Francisco. One of the first things I did after walking into the Californios kitchen was help make the agua fresca. Californios is a very special place that captures all the coolness of the Bay Area and celebrates the glorious bounty of Mexican culinary and agricultural resources. The aguas at Californios change seasonally. When I was interning, I helped make a stone fruit agua fresca with mint tea, sweetened with agave. The restaurant's aguas have intricate steps one would expect from a fine-dining establishment: Pristine stone fruit is juiced with just the right amount of agave and a blend of California teas. The addition of tea into agua fresca adds a beautiful herbal note.

SERVES 8

4 chamomile tea bags

1 Bosc pear, cut into large chunks

1 cup strawberries, hulled

¼ cup agave nectar

Ice for serving

In a large saucepan, combine 8 cups of water and tea bags and bring to a gentle simmer over high heat. Once simmering, cover, remove from the heat, and let steep for 15 minutes. Discard the tea bags, pour the tea into a container, and stick it in the freezer until cool, about 45 minutes.

In a blender, combine the pear, strawberries, and 1 cup of the cooled tea. Blend the mixture for 1 minute, or until it is a rough puree. Strain through a fine-mesh sieve into a large pitcher, discarding the solids. Add the rest of the cooled tea and the agave. Let chill in the fridge for at least 10 minutes. To serve, fill glasses with ice and pour the agua over the ice. Store any leftovers in the fridge for up to 3 days.

FROZEN LIME AGUAS

Aguas are another blessing from ancient Mexico. There are so many fun and tasty regional Mexican variations, from seeds (sesame, chia) to herbs (mint, basil, epazote), from fruits (strawberry, pineapple, any variety of melon, cucumbers, guava, lemon, lime) and calyx (hibiscus) to less common veggies (beets). Of course, these flavors don't need to stand alone and can be mixed. Some of my favorites are Jamaica and pineapple (see page 180), cucumber and mint, and epazote and lime. I suggest using Mexican limes, which can be juicier than other limes, but there are endless options and combinations for your choice of aguas. The traditional process for this is to mash fruit with some sweetener. If you chose a thick sweetener substitute such as honey, agave, or even a boiled, unrefined compact sugar, like piloncillo, I suggest mixing it with a bit of warm water first so it can easily dissolve. While bits of pulp are common in aguas, clumps of sugar are not!

SERVES 4

⅓ cup lime juice (5 to 6 limes)

⅓ cup natural cane sugar

3 cups of ice (about 24 ice cubes)

½ cup water

In a blender, combine the juice, sugar, and ice. Blend the mixture on high until it resembles a sorbet. If there are still chunks of ice, turn the blender off and give the mixture a quick stir. Once all chunks are gone, turn the blender back on high and slowly drizzle in the water until it resembles a slushy texture. Serve right after blending and enjoy!

SUN CHAI

Ethiopia has a drink named shai, which is "tea" in Amharic. It is very similar to masala chai. It is really intriguing to me that the Sanskrit and Hindi words for tea are both *chai*. Ethiopia and India share an ancient past that goes back two thousand years. While Ethiopia has never been colonized, they have kept Ethiopian traditions as a closely guarded historical legacy. This is similar to the way the Indian government created the Quality Council of India to certify Ayurvedic products. In India, masala chai first gained prominence as an Ayurvedic healing drink. The ever-constant reverence for traditional medicine in my own upbringing makes Ayurvedic products embedded in my memories. From as early as I can remember, I would scoop heaping spoonfuls of herbal mixtures like chyawanprash into my mouth as if I was gulping down the yummiest of jams. I loved drinking a nut milk version of golden milk. But my favorite was masala chai. This ancient drink has evolved over the years to include black tea leaves and milk. In this recipe, I like how the sun transforms these ingredients into something subtle yet flavorful. When the tea is infused in the sun, it has a unique flavor with a pleasant warmth. I created this recipe without dairy to celebrate the wonderful spices of chai.

SERVES 8

2 star anise pods

1 teaspoon whole cloves

9 green cardamom pods

1 (1-inch) piece ginger

1 (3-inch) cinnamon stick

2 tablespoons loose-leaf black tea (or 6 black tea bags), preferably Nepali or Assam

8 cups distilled water

Ice for serving (optional)

Any kind of sweetener, such as agave nectar or honey, for serving (optional)

In a molcajete or other mortar and pestle, pound together the star anise, cloves, cardamom, ginger, cinnamon, and tea until coarsely ground, with a small amount of powder at the bottom.

In a large pitcher, combine the spices and tea with the water. Cover the pitcher with a lid or plastic wrap and leave in a sunny spot for at least 4 hours and up to 6 hours, then strain. I do not recommend going beyond 6 hours. To serve cold, pour the chai into glasses filled with ice. To serve hot, pour the tea into a saucepan over medium heat and bring to a gentle simmer. Sweeten it if you like.

SPICED CIDER

Haitian and Mexican foodways are renowned for their cinnamon teas. This apple cider recipe was inspired by the Haitian tea, which has gentle star anise flavors, and the Mexican tea, which celebrates cinnamon flavors with an infusion from whole cinnamon sticks. The hint of orange in this recipes gives a great aroma to the cider and helps balance the sweet and spicy flavors.

SERVES 4

5 Gala apples (2 to 2½ pounds), cored and cut into 8 slices

1 navel orange, halved

3 (3-inch) cinnamon sticks

2 star anise pods

¼ cup light brown sugar

8 cups water

In a large stockpot over high heat, add the apple slices, orange halves, cinnamon, star anise, brown sugar, and eight cups of water. Cover the pot and bring to a boil, stirring every so often to dissolve the sugar, about 10 minutes. Once the pot is boiling, decrease the heat to low and bring to a gentle simmer for 90 minutes, stirring occasionally to make sure the water hasn't reduced too quickly. Once done, the apple skin should look pale, and the apple pieces should be soft. Using a slotted spoon, remove the orange halves. Mash the apples until they are no larger than half an inch. Strain them through a fine-mesh sieve into a large pitcher, by slightly pressing the apples to gently push out the liquid. Save what's left in the sieve to add to smoothies or eat as an applesauce. Let the cider cool for about 5 minutes or until you're able to comfortably drink it.

OAT HORCHATA

In the Mexican tradition, horchata is often made from soaked rice and almonds. Horchata made only with rice is called horchata de arroz. In Puerto Rico, horchata de ajonjolí is made with soaked, finely ground toasted sesame seeds. Other variations use ground melon seeds or serve horchata with flowers and fruit. Horchata came to Mexico by way of Spanish and Portuguese colonialism. Before going to Mexico, it was brought to Europe through African influence. In Nigeria, it is called kunnu aya, which is most likely the original form of the drink. In this case, *kunnu aya* is literally the word for tigernuts, which offer a great source of protein. It makes sense to me, as original African culinary expressions are almost always tied to beneficial nutritional outcomes. The ironic thing about nuts and rice being used as a substitute for the tigernut is that the tigernut isn't a nut at all. It is a tuber, like ginger and turmeric. My version is also nut free, which has the added benefit of being quicker, since it doesn't require the typical overnight soak for the almonds. My intention in this recipe is to infuse a lot of flavor without a lot of time.

SERVES 4

½ cup short-grain brown rice or long-grain white rice

½ cup rolled oats

1 (3-inch) cinnamon stick

⅓ cup agave nectar

4 cups cold water

Ice for serving

In a blender, combine the rice, oats, and cinnamon and blend for 15 to 30 seconds, until you get a fine powder. Turn the blender off and add the agave and water. Blend the horchata for about 30 seconds, until well combined. Strain the mixture through a fine-mesh sieve lined with cheesecloth or a kitchen towel and into a pitcher, squeezing out as much liquid as you can and discarding the leftover slurry. Serve over ice and enjoy! Store leftovers in the refrigerator for up to 4 days.

NEW ORLEANS–STYLE VIETNAMESE ICED COFFEE

This recipe is all about infusion. From the coffee grounds to the milk, we add flavor notes that enhance and embrace the natural coffee flavors. My favorite memories of iced coffee include making it with grounds from Cafe du Monde, a coffee brand from Louisiana that includes chicory. Chicory has been used since ancient times by the Egyptians for medicinal purposes. In Louisiana, historically chicory was much cheaper than coffee and was used as a filler, by itself or with parsnips, to create a coffeelike drink. The taste is warm and bitter like coffee, but with nutty, woody notes. I love the Vietnamese styles of roasting coffee and wanted to incorporate the chicory to reflect the Vietnamese contributions to New Orleans coffee culture.

SERVES 2

3 tablespoons ground chicory-infused coffee

1 tablespoon dried chicory

1 cup milk, any fat percentage, or 2 cups unsweetened almond milk

⅔ cup natural cane sugar

1 cinnamon stick

1 cup ice

Using your preferred method, brew the coffee grounds and chicory with 3 cups of water. Let the coffee cool in the freezer.

In a skillet that's at least 12 inches wide, combine the milk, sugar, and cinnamon. Bring to a simmer over medium-high heat, stirring until the sugar dissolves. Let reduce over low heat for 45 to 50 minutes without stirring, until the milk looks thick and glossy with an almost pale yellow tint. (If you're making vegan condensed milk, you're looking for a thick texture and grayish color.) At the end, with a spoon, gently remove the cinnamon stick and any foam from the surface.

Take the coffee out of the freezer and add 2 tablespoons of the condensed milk. Divide the ice between two glasses, then divide the cold coffee between them and serve. Store leftover condensed milk, covered, in the fridge for up to a week. (The vegan condensed milk will thicken in the fridge more than the dairy condensed milk, so you may have to microwave it for 15 to 30 seconds to get a pourable consistency again.)

8-HOUR COLD BREW

My love for coffee is similar to my love for baked goods. I love all varieties and never want to choose just one. Northern California is a celebrated home for artisan Black- and Brown-owned coffee roasters. My favorite roasters are Proyecto Diaz and Red Bay Coffee. The Bay Area used to be one of the three main ports for coffee importing, with sizeable commercial coffee roasting production. But the flavor and fair-trade considerations of small coffee roasters and importers eventually became mainstream and celebrated. Before all of this, Bay Area coffee culture originated in 1850 as a result of the Gold Rush population boom. It is well known that many wildly successful coffee brands came from Californian coffee roasters. I like to set this cold brew up in the morning, after breakfast, so when I get done with my day I can filter it and have it over the next few days.

SERVES 4

⅔ cup whole coffee beans

In a coffee grinder, coarsely grind the coffee to resemble a rocky sand texture. In a pitcher or large jar, combine the coffee grounds and 6 cups of cold water. Cover the container and let it steep in the fridge for at least 8 hours and up to 12 hours. Strain through a fine-mesh sieve lined with cheesecloth or a kitchen towel into another large jar or pitcher, repeating as necessary to remove any chalky coffee bean solids. Once the liquid has been strained, discard the coffee grounds or save them for compost. Serve however you like your coffee, or store in the fridge for up to a week.

FRENCH QUARTER FROZEN COFFEE

Oftentimes when I'm sitting in a café, bakery, or restaurant, I am not just admiring their decorations. I'm actively watching the staff's techniques and methods in making my favorite things. So, when I fell in love with the frozen coffees found in the French Quarter of New Orleans, I knew I had to try to replicate them at home. I wanted to achieve something that had body but still had liquid and didn't end up as a frozen icy water mass devoid of coffee flavor. While I sat and watched the staff take the coffee concentrate and pour it through a slush machine, I knew I had to come up with an option that my good old trusty blender could create. To make this recipe a bit quicker, keep frozen coffee cubes in your freezer so you can have them ready when you want to start the recipe next time.

SERVES 3

1½ cups brewed coffee

3 tablespoons natural cane sugar

½ cup milk, any kind

Fill an ice cube tray with the coffee. Let it freeze overnight, or until solid. Add the coffee ice cubes, sugar, and milk to a blender. Slowly blend the ingredients, starting with the lowest setting and working your way up to the highest, until mostly smooth. This may take several minutes, depending on the strength of your blender, and a tamper can help speed along the process. Turn off the blender and use a rubber spatula to stir the coffee. If the coffee ice is still not completely blended, use the spatula to push the ice to the bottom and continue blending until smooth. Serve in pint glasses and enjoy before it melts!

Pantry Basics —— 7

This chapter focuses on pantry essentials that can help you navigate the kitchen easily and efficiently. All the seasonings in this chapter are used throughout this book and are really helpful to have on hand. I love to keep extra jerk seasoning around to season toast, chips, popcorn, and almost any snack. The creole seasoning and berbere are both super versatile as well. I use the creole seasoning for quick things like oven-roasted fries and sautéed vegetables, but in the book, I've also included my favorite uses of it, like in the Breakfast Potatoes with Crispy Fried Herbs and Garlic (page 33) and Cornflour Panfried Fish (page 133).

My favorite thing about stock is making use of all the random scraps and "unusable" items in my kitchen. The crab stock is flavored solely from crab. For vegetable stock, all you need is some water and any leftover vegetables.

HERBY INFUSED OIL

This recipe is entirely editable; and I highly recommend it. I call for extra-virgin olive oil, but you can substitute any of your favorite oils. When it comes to the aromatics (garlic, oregano, and lemon), you could sub them with serrano peppers and fresh thyme, dried chiles with ginger, or any combo of your choice. Infused oil is a great way to use leftover bits that might be too spicy or pungent to go into a stock but that aren't ready for the compost bin yet. I love infused oils for finishing soups and purees, or in salad dressings and marinades. When working at Chez Panisse, a classic California restaurant in Berkeley, I would often make infused oils for duck or lamb marinades, using anything from lemon peel and oregano to cumin seeds and pounded green garlic. You can't really go wrong with your favorite flavor combos and arrangements.

MAKES 1 CUP

1 cup extra-virgin olive oil

1 garlic clove, crushed

2 sprigs oregano

1 (1-inch) piece lemon peel

In a saucepan, heat the olive oil over medium heat until warm, about 3 minutes. In a jar, combine the garlic, oregano, and lemon peel. Slowly pour the warm oil over the contents of your jar. Let the oil sit for at least 15 minutes, until the oil takes on the flavors of the ingredients. You will know when this happens by smell or, when cooled, by taste. Store, with the aromatics still in the oil, for up to 1 week in the fridge.

COMPOUND BUTTER

The origins of any recipe can be complicated and come with strong points of contention. I shy away from ideas of ownership when it comes to the natural world, but we should question why some things are attributed to a single culture. Butter is a great example. You may have heard that compound butter is a classic European technique, but butter originated some eight thousand years ago in ancient Africa, so it would be naïve—and most likely inaccurate— to attribute compound butter to Europe alone.

Compound butter is an easy way to infuse extra flavor into butter itself and the dish you are preparing. This recipe is a classic compound butter that uses fresh herbs and garlic. Feel free to experiment with dry seasonings, roasted vegetables, or even citrus zest. As the butter sits, more flavor is incorporated. So, on the first day you make this recipe, the taste might not be as strong as it will be a few days later.

MAKES ½ CUP

½ cup (1 stick) unsalted butter, at room temperature

Leaves from 2 sprigs thyme (around 2 tablespoons), minced

Leaves from 2 sprigs rosemary, minced

2 garlic cloves, minced

Run the outside of a bowl under hot water for about 30 seconds, making sure no water gets inside the bowl. This will help soften the butter and make it easier to incorporate the herbs. Place the butter in the warmed bowl along with the thyme, rosemary, and garlic. Mash together all of the ingredients with a fork until thoroughly combined. If you would like to shape the butter or make it more uniform, you can place it in plastic wrap and roll it into a log shape or put it into a mold and place it in the fridge to set the shape. Store in a sealed container in the fridge for up to the expiration date on the butter carton, which is normally 2 to 3 weeks.

VEGGIE STOCK

Vegetable stock is one of the best ways to reduce food waste at home. I find that keeping a bowl on the counter to collect vegetable scraps throughout the week helps to create the base for veggie stock. I place it in the fridge when I am done with the food prep at each meal. This recipe is a general guide for making stock, so feel free to use 3 cups of whatever vegetables you have on hand, taking care to limit bitter-tasting vegetables—such as the end portions of kale, radishes, and arugula—to no more than 1 cup. If all you have are bitter ends of things, I sometimes add an apple or pear to balance out the flavor. How you use your stock depends on what you put in it: If you have ginger and onion scraps, think about turning your stock into pho. If you have extra thyme and rosemary stem scraps, your stock might be perfect for clam chowder, veggie minestrone, or chicken noodle soup.

MAKES 4 CUPS

1 carrot, cut into 2-inch pieces

2 celery stalks, cut into 2-inch pieces

1 onion, cut into 2-inch pieces

1 green bell pepper, cut into 2-inch pieces

In a stockpot, combine 6 cups of water, carrot, celery, onion, and bell pepper and bring to a simmer over high heat. (This should take around 15 minutes.) Once the pot is simmering, lower the heat to medium and simmer for 30 more minutes. The liquid should be fragrant and tinged brown. Strain or scoop out the veggies and store them in the fridge for soups such as veggie minestrone and chicken noodle soup. Store the stock in a covered container for up to a week in the fridge. You can also freeze the stock and thaw when needed.

CRAB STOCK

While the king crab may be more prized and therefore more expensive, I am partial to the Dungeness crab. The whole crab can seem intimidating, but I assure you this technique isn't super demanding or convoluted. This recipe was inspired by my internship at Mister Jiu's in San Francisco. I love the restaurant, and I really respect the way owner and chef Brandon Jew runs his kitchen. On one of my days working there, the most fragrant smelling seafood stock was gently bubbling. When I thought of my pantry contents, I immediately knew I wanted to create my own version. This recipe does call for some active time at the stove, but there is a considerable amount of inactive time when you can relax and wait on this deliciousness. The crab broth is subtly sweet and filled with rich umami flavors.

MAKES 6 CUPS

5 quarts distilled or spring water

1 live crab (about 2 pounds)

In a stockpot, bring the water to a boil over high heat. While you wait, leave the crab in the fridge or cooler, as the cool air helps sedate or relax the crab. Once the water is boiling, drop in the crab, head first, and cook for 10 minutes. Remove the crab and place it in a container in the fridge. See the Cook's Note (opposite) for how to break down the crab while your stock reduces. Keep boiling down the leftover water, uncovered, until it reduces to 6 cups of stock. This should take about 1 hour.

COOK'S NOTE: HOW TO BREAK DOWN A COOKED CRAB

Remove each leg and claw from the crab with a gentle twist. Now take the legs and separate each into two pieces: Using a crab cracker (or a kitchen towel folded around the crab piece), apply pressure to the leg. Once the shell cracks, peel it apart, remove the meat, and place the meat in a bowl. It's important to check for small shell pieces that may have found their way into your lump meat, so be careful and go slowly. Repeat with the remaining legs and claws. For the body, remove the large top shell. Remove the off-white gills, which are inedible. You will also find the digestive gland that is usually yellow-white or greenish. It is known by various names, like tomalley, crab fat, or crab butter. You can just throw it away, but it is very popular in NorCal to eat with crackers or small toast bites. (It can contain a natural toxin called domoic acid, which can be harmful to some.) Flip the crab over and remove the triangular flap, known as the apron. Crack the white center body in half to reveal the crabmeat. Pick out the meat, continuing to collect it in the bowl while discarding the shells. Store the crabmeat in an airtight container in the fridge for up to 3 days.

CREOLE SEASONING

Creole means many different things. It can refer to a dish made with the Louisianan flavor base of celery, bell pepper, and onion, known as the holy trinity. It can be even more subtle and refer to food that has simply been seasoned with creole seasoning. Commonly, creole seasoning uses at least three peppers (white, black, and cayenne) to ensure complex, robust flavor. This recipe still adheres to that rule, but I selected chile powder, paprika, and black pepper as my three. The black pepper and chile powder add spice, while the paprika adds color and smoky, sweet, spicy flavor. Many commercial creole seasonings are around 50% salt and 50% peppers and herbs. This can be a little too salty for some people. My recipe uses only a quarter teaspoon of salt to showcase the flavors in the spice mix. This seasoning adds a great flavor to most dishes and can create that cooked-all-day taste. It works well in a variety of dishes, like hash, gumbo, and humble roasted vegetables. I like to use a bit to season my movie-night popcorn, too.

MAKES ¼ CUP

6 garlic cloves

1 tablespoon dried oregano

1 tablespoon fresh thyme leaves (from about 1 sprig)

1 tablespoon chile powder

1 teaspoon paprika

1 teaspoon freshly ground black pepper

¼ teaspoon fine sea salt

Preheat the oven to 250°F. Line a baking sheet with parchment paper or a silicone mat. Grate the garlic, then spread the garlic out onto the prepared baking sheet and bake for 15 minutes, or until lightly browned. If the garlic sticks to the parchment paper, lift it off delicately with a spatula.

Meanwhile, combine the oregano, thyme, chile powder, paprika, and pepper in a skillet. Over medium heat, toast the seasonings until the smell starts to waft through the air, about 5 minutes. In a spice grinder, gently pulse together the toasted seasonings, garlic, and salt. The creole seasoning can last for some time in a dry space in your pantry. I like to store my spices in small glass jars, but in a pinch I will use a plastic reusable bag. Clumping is natural after three months or so, and we know this is one of the reasons why commercial spice mixtures use preservatives. It does not mean your spices have gone bad; just use a fork to break up any clumps to ensure your spices are evenly distributed in the dish.

JERK SEASONING

We know that jerk originated as an underground cooking tradition with a specific seasoning. It uses the barbacoa cooking technique commonly associated with Mexican culture, but in this case was developed by the indigenous Jamaican people, the Taíno. There was an ancient relationship between the indigenous people in Mexico, like the Aztecs and Mayans, and the Taíno, so tracing the culinary origins of barbacoa is complicated, especially if you add that barbecue originated from barbacoa, and Haitians lay claim to those origins. The jerk technique used by the Coromantee people of Jamaica, who are also known as Maroons, allowed them to cook and be self-sufficient without revealing their location to murderous colonialists from England. They live in the mountainous Cockpit Country, in Jamaica, which is considered remote and challenging to travel to even in modern times. Typically, foods made from this technique are cooked low, slow, and with pimento wood. Within Jamaica, there are so many regional expressions of jerk.

Nowadays, restaurant jerk preparation is often done on a grill. Jerk works best when a marinade is transformed by caramelization. Commercial jerk spice seasonings, like Walkerswood and Grace, are often found in a wet rub marinade form. But I love a dry brine over a wet one, so I wanted to make a dry jerk seasoning recipe that could be more versatile. While some may associate jerk with pork or chicken, my earliest memories of it involve salmon, shrimp, eggplant, and tofu. Try the quick, tasty Jerk Eggplant Steaks (page 121).

MAKES ABOUT ¾ CUP

3 tablespoons light brown sugar

2 tablespoons garlic powder

2 tablespoons chile powder

2 tablespoons dried oregano

2 tablespoons onion powder

1 tablespoon smoked paprika

1 tablespoon freshly ground black pepper

1 tablespoon fine sea salt

1 teaspoon ground nutmeg

1 teaspoon ground cumin

1 teaspoon ground allspice

In a skillet, combine the garlic powder, nutmeg, chile powder, oregano, paprika, cumin, onion powder, allspice, and black pepper. Toast the spices over medium heat, stirring occasionally, for about 4 minutes, until the spices have slightly darkened and the smells permeate the air. Transfer the spices to an airtight container and let cool. Stir in the brown sugar and salt. Store in a cool, dry place for up to 6 months.

BERBERE SEASONING

Berbere seasoning is so versatile. I really recommend doubling this recipe so that you have it on hand to add to breakfast hash, scrambled tofu, or eggs, a dinner main dish, or really anything that you want to infuse with great flavor quickly. When working with dry spices, it is helpful to avoid spillage or inaccurate measurements by measuring spices individually and then pouring each of those smaller amounts into a larger container. Berbere has a unique flavor of warm spices, and when it is stewed into dishes or sprinkled into salads, the taste is remarkable. A good number of Ethiopian and Eritrean dishes use berbere liberally. Sometimes it can be challenging to find berbere packaged in amounts higher than one or two tablespoons. I recommend making the recipe from scratch or buying from a spice-specific shop. Costwise, I think homemade is the way to go. Most of the spices in this recipe might already be in your cabinet! If you're at a loss to find the ground chile California, try New Mexico chile or look for it at grocery stores specializing in Mexican foods. If all you find is the whole dried chile, you can remove the stem and seeds and grind it yourself in a spice grinder or blender.

MAKES ABOUT ⅓ CUP

2 tablespoons onion powder

1 tablespoon smoked paprika

1 tablespoon ground chile California

1 teaspoon ground coriander

1 teaspoon ground fenugreek

1 teaspoon freshly ground black pepper

½ teaspoon ground cinnamon

½ teaspoon ground cardamom

½ teaspoon ground ginger

½ teaspoon ground nutmeg

¼ teaspoon ground allspice

Heat a small saucepan over medium heat. Add the onion powder, paprika, chile California, coriander, fenugreek, ground pepper, cinnamon, cardamom, ginger, and nutmeg and toast for 4 to 5 minutes, until the mixture slightly deepens in color and the smell permeates the air. Cool and store in an airtight container for up to 6 months. I like glass jars for spices because you can easily see what is inside and I feel it keeps ingredients drier than other options.

CORN FLOUR

Corn has so many uses. In this book, the Cornflour Panfried Fish (page 129) and the Corn Cakes (page 37) are great ways to use corn flour. Native people in what is now Mexico and the US have many wonderful corn-related recipes such as cookies, savory corn cakes, pozole hominy soup, sweet cakes, and grits. There is a long-standing connection between Black culinary tradition and Native American indigenous foods. Native and Black people were the original cultivators of land, resources, and America's economy. This recipe is an act of respect and acknowledgment of how and why we have certain ingredients today.

Corn flour is usually made from dried white corn kernels, but popcorn kernels are an easy substitute. Speaking of substitutions, I like the cornbread variations that use corn flour instead of all-purpose flour. This recipe uses only one ingredient and a few kitchen tools. You can buy corn flour from the store, but this is super simple and the taste is phenomenal in comparison.

MAKES ABOUT 3 CUPS

2 cups popcorn kernels

Place the popcorn kernels in a blender. On the highest setting, blend the popcorn for 1 minute. Mix around the popcorn kernels with a wooden spoon to make sure you don't overheat your blender, and also examine the state of the kernels. If you have a powerful high-speed blender, your kernels might already resemble a powdery flour. If not, blend them again for 1 minute. You are looking for a smooth flour without any kernel chunks or bits. Off of the blender base, mix with a wooden spoon to examine, and if need be, blend it for another minute.

Place a fine-mesh sieve over a bowl and pour the contents of the blender into the sieve. Let all the powdery corn flour fall through. You might need to do this process three times. Each blender has different power levels, and some might work faster or slower. Place the remaining coarse bits into a separate container and use later whenever you make corn flour again. (The prechopped pieces will help the blending process for next time.) Place your corn flour into a sealed container and store it on a dry, cool shelf for up to several months.

CORN TORTILLAS

The tortilla can become a meal unto itself, and the corn tortilla is an extra special thing. While there are a multitude of ways to eat corn tortillas—for example, as tacos and quesadillas, which are so much better when made with a fresh tortilla—I prefer a straightforward approach. When I was younger, I would heat a corn tortilla on an open flame and eat it with butter, maybe a sliver of avocado, and hot sauce. Either that, or I'd just eat it plain. (In fact, I still love eating plain charred corn tortillas.) In this book, I've included a mole verde taco recipe (see page 122) that is delicious when used with this fragrant tortilla. Bring out your tortilla press if you have one on hand, otherwise, use a rolling pin.

Masa is corn that has gone through a scientifically complex alkaline preparation called nixtamalization, created by the Aztecs. Masa, especially masa made from organic or heirloom corn, is naturally so rich and sweet that the taste is unparalleled. Organic masa may be challenging to find, but it is worth seeking out as an ethical way to preserve foodways, which benefits the earth and future generations. Preserving cultural diversity is directly proportional to preserving ecological diversity.

I love cooking tortillas. I find it very relaxing. The warm smell that wraps around the kitchen when masa meets the skillet or comal is soothing. When I was fifteen, I did an internship with Chef Ray Garcia at Broken Spanish in Los Angeles. The tortillas at Broken Spanish and its taqueria, B.S. Taqueria, were always so delicious. I spent part of my time meticulously weighing out and rolling the highest quality masa and cooking hundreds of tortillas alongside a cook nicknamed Máquina ("machine"). Máquina cooked the tortillas on the comal with super speed and technique. Just watching him work showed me what not to do and what to do to consistently create tortillas with perfection. I learned a lot at Broken Spanish, and it made me think of my early memories of my mom and grandma making corn tortillas. So much of cooking is, like any other science, grounded in respectful observation.

MAKES 4 TO 6 TORTILLAS

1 cup organic masa harina

Place the masa harina in a small mixing bowl. Slowly pour ¼ cup of water into the bowl. With a wooden spoon, mix the masa until the water has absorbed. Pour in another ¼ cup of water, stir again with the wooden spoon, and press the mixture against the bowl with your spoon to eliminate any lumps. Continue stirring

continued

until the masa resembles a children's playdough; it should be able to be formed and hold a shape (this step might take a few minutes). If the dough is still dry, add up to 2 tablespoons more water. Cover your bowl with plastic wrap or a kitchen towel. Let the dough rest at room temperature for 20 minutes.

Once the dough has rested, place two pieces of plastic wrap or parchment paper to fit inside of a tortilla press. If you're rolling the tortillas by hand, place the plastic directly on a work surface. Heat a cast-iron skillet or a comal over medium heat.

While the skillet is heating up, roll 2 full tablespoons of masa into a ball, open the tortilla press, and place the masa ball between the two pieces of plastic. Gently press the tortilla out to approximately the thickness of a quarter by closing the tortilla press and applying uniform gentle pressure for 10 seconds. Make sure there is no plastic wrapped around the top of your press so the plastic isn't sticking to the tortillas. When you lift the top of the tortilla press to release the tortilla, don't let the tortilla or plastic wrap lift, too. If you don't have a tortilla press, sandwich a ball of masa between the two small pieces of plastic wrap on your work surface and, using a rolling pin, bottle, or glass jar, roll the ball out into a 4- to 5-inch circle.

Remove the top layer of plastic from the tortilla. Place the tortilla directly onto your hand or the skillet or comal and remove the other piece of plastic. Cook the tortilla for 3 minutes, flipping halfway through. You are looking for a pliable texture but not a char or cooked look to the tortilla. Wrap the tortilla in a kitchen towel to keep warm. Repeat with the remaining masa.

Serve immediately, or allow the tortillas to cool before placing them in the fridge. Warm tortillas can create condensation and moisture that will encourage spoilage. They can be wrapped in a kitchen towel, aluminum foil, parchment paper, or placed in a plastic reusable bag and refrigerated for up to a week. Just remember, the longer the tortilla is stored in the fridge, the less pliable it will be. The freshest tortillas are best for tacos and flautas, while older tortillas are better for chips, enchiladas, and tostadas.

continued

Cook's Note: To reheat these tortillas or any packaged variety, wrap 8 tortillas in aluminum foil and place in a preheated oven at 325°F for 20 to 25 minutes. Yes, the oven method is slower than the microwave, but it provides gentler heating that allows the tortillas to steam. You can also reheat them on the stove top, but the temperature will be lower, and should be done in batches of 2 or 3.

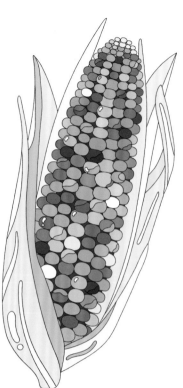

ESCABECHE

Escabeche is a gift from Moorish Spain to the world. Its expression in Mexico resulted in a spicy pickled arrangement of vegetables usually made up of cauliflower, carrots, and radishes. I chose to make this recipe with solely radishes for a variety of reasons. Unless you're operating a whole restaurant, or eat escabeche every day, a whole head of cauliflower, a carrot, and a bunch of radishes might be too many pickles for the average person. So, I went with my favorite part of escabeche, the radishes. You can add or remove any vegetable from this recipe, but I love radishes' earthy flavor and snappy texture. Use escabeche as a taco topping or just as a side to add a bit of spice and acid to any meal.

MAKES ONE 16-OUNCE JAR

1 bunch radishes

1 tablespoon extra-virgin olive oil

1 serrano pepper, halved

1 teaspoon dried oregano

1 teaspoon fine sea salt

2 garlic cloves, crushed

2 cups spring water

½ cup apple cider vinegar

1 teaspoon natural cane sugar

Clean the radishes and remove the tops and bottoms. Cut the radishes in half lengthwise, then cut thin slices to make half-moons. Place the radishes in a 16-ounce mason jar. In a saucepan, combine the oil, serrano pepper, oregano, salt, and garlic and heat over high heat. Cook for about 2 minutes, stirring occasionally, until the garlic and serrano are slightly browned. Add the water, vinegar, and sugar and bring to a boil. Pour this pickling liquid over the radishes. Seal the jar and place it in the fridge for at least 15 minutes or up to 10 days.

Acknowledgments

Huge thank-you to the entire team that helped make *Flavor+Us* possible. Thank you, Danielle Svetcov, my literary agent, who sold my book and supported me the entire way. Danielle has an infectious charm that I greatly admire.

Thanks to my mentor Bryant Terry who has supported my journey from the day I met him when I was thirteen years old. Thanks for always being a call away to help with advice when I was dealing with completely new experiences in the food world.

Thank you to Amanda Yee, who always keeps it real. Thanks so much for everything you've done over the years. From supporting me from another country, flying across the country to help me with my first-ever cookbook shoot, and most importantly, showing me how to lead people with respect, grace, and authority.

Thank you to Kelly Snowden and Claire Yee, the editors who always work with such kindness and helped bring my story to life. Thank you to Betsy Stromberg for your time and dedication to making this book beautiful. Thanks to Emily Timberlake, who went through my entire manuscript, pulling out stories and meaning with the utmost care and consideration.

Thanks so much to food stylists Lillian Kang and Paige Arnett, prop stylist Jillian Knox, and photographer Ed Anderson. I was beyond nervous to do a full book photo shoot. Lillian, Paige, Jillian, and Ed were the best team and created one of the best-ever set environments. The way these four work with such precision, beauty, and care really inspired me.

Thank you to my recipe tester, Janelle Bitker, who I immediately hired after hearing she could be a tester for this book. Getting to know Janelle for the past five years has been so great, from meeting her during an interview back in 2018, judging dishes at the Oakland A's stadium together, reading her amazing work, and now working together. Janelle put the most time and effort into these recipes, all while being the senior editor of the *San Francisco Chronicle*'s Food & Wine section. I truly couldn't imagine doing this without her amazing expertise.

Thank you so much to my family.

My grandparents Jean Bisseret and Velia Martinez. Who showed me the amazing way that our family can persevere through anything. Who were brave enough to create a family of different races and religions in 1969, only two years after interracial marriages were legalized. Thank you, Grandpa Jean, who journeyed from Haiti to America to work in film editing at CBS and showed me the balance of language, hard work, and life's joys.

Thank you, Grandma Velia, who would sing me and my sisters to sleep in English and Spanish every night we visited, and carry us to the kitchen for breakfast in the morning. Who always secured my sisters and my identities as Black and Mexican girls at a time when we were the only ones I knew of.

Thank you to my mom, Mona, who not only taught me almost everything I know and raised her children in a radical way to understand race and identity as young as possible, and to see the beauty in our cultures and environments. Thank you, Mom, for instilling the importance of literacy and taking me to the library every week growing up. Thank you to my cool older sisters, Gabriella, Summaya, and Fidela, who are always there to talk and give advice. Thanks for always being the people I could go to laugh, cry, and rant.

Thanks to Coach Terry and Iesha, who have taught me so much on and off the court. Thanks for helping mold me over the years into a better person, tennis player, and tennis coach.

Thanks so much to Julia Turshen, who has always been an inspiration over the years. Thanks for all the calls and advice, especially when I was pitching my cookbook. Thanks for teaching me the importance of my story and how that is enough for a cookbook proposal. Thank you, Julia and Grace Bonney, for reading my cookbook proposal and helping me mold it into a better version each time.

Thank you to Alice Waters, who I first met during a book signing at thirteen and who would invite me to become an intern at Chez Panisse and offer me a job in the restaurant three years later. Thank you for taking a chance on the nervous middle schooler whose world you influenced and changed for the better. Thank you for sharing your joy and knowledge with children and adults all over the world.

Thanks to Chef Amy Dencler, who hired me as a prep cook at eighteen. Thank you to Chef Amy and Chef Cedric Tolosa, and the Panisse family, who taught me so much about beautifully delicious food and what a work environment should be like, for cheering me on when I was finishing this book, graduating from high school, and leaving for college. Thanks for the laughs, lessons, and experiences.

Thanks, Curtis Stone, for always supporting my dream, the beauty that is Gwen, and reminding me to finish school.

Thank you to Hawa Hassan for teaching me not only to invest in my business but in the wellness of myself.

Thank you to Guy Fieri for not only lessons from winning *Guy's Grocery Games*, but most importantly, going on a walk with me after I lost the second time around, talking to me and showing me the ways hospitality is expressed throughout the food industry.

Thank you, Jeremy Chan and the team at Ikoyi, for teaching me how to make a quenelle and then, twenty minutes later, letting me plate the pastry for the rest of the night. Thank you for encouraging me to go to college and teaching me about how rewarding a career in food can be.

Thank you to my godmother Adrian Lipscombe, who has been so amazing to know through the years. Thank you for your compassion, understanding, and for being someone who showed me there is always a solution or resolve for any problem.

Thanks to all my teachers over the years who allowed me into their business kitchens and chef libraries, and took the time to work with me directly (Shirley Chung, Nina Compton, Emeril Lagasse, Vallery Lomas, Ryan Shelton, Reem Assil, Tiffany Derry, Brandon Jew, Melissa Chou, Sean Walsh, Sachiko, Hugo Alejandro Bolanos, and Thérèse Nelson).

Thank you to Toni Morrision, whose life and legacy led the way for this book.

About the Contributors

Rahanna Bisseret Martinez began cooking in Northern California when she was six years old. She was the second-place finisher on season one of *Top Chef Junior*. After the show, Rahanna chose to continue her culinary education and serve in the hospitality community. She interned around the culinary world—at Wolfgang Puck at Hotel Bel-Air, Emeril's, Compère Lapin, Californios, Tartine Bakery, Mister Jiu's, Ikoyi, and more—before deciding to work at Chez Panisse. Rahanna has also showcased her recipes in the *New York Times, San Francisco Chronicle*, NBC *Today, Teen Vogue*, and many others. Her writing can also be found in *Black Food*, edited by Bryant Terry. Rahanna currently lives in Ithaca, New York, where she attends Cornell University studying hotel administration.

Ed Anderson is a food and travel photographer with a particular love of cookbooks . . . and overcast days. He lives with his family in Northern California.

Index

Typefaces: Monotype's Ionic No 5, The Northern Block's Moret, and TypeType's TT Wellingtons

Library of Congress Cataloging-in-Publication Data
    Names: Bisseret Martinez, Rahanna, 2004- author. | Anderson, Ed (Edward
        Charles), photographer.
    Title: Flavor+us : cooking for everyone / Rahanna Bisseret Martinez ;
        photography by Ed Anderson.
    Other titles: Flavor plus us
    Description: California : Ten Speed Press, [2023] | In title, "plus"
        appears as a plus sign (+). | Summary: "In Flavor + Us, Top Chef Junior
        finalist Rahanna Bisseret Martinez seeks to connect cooking methods
        around the world in a way that is fun and inclusive for all cooks at all
        levels. Throughout her recipes, Rahanna highlights techniques that make
        these dishes shine, creating a book that welcomes cuisines from all
        around the world to the table and that acknowledges how much we can
        learn from kitchens of others"— Provided by publisher.
    Identifiers: LCCN 2022034805 (print) | LCCN 2022034806 (ebook) | ISBN
        9781984860569 (hardcover) | ISBN 9781984860576 (ebook)
    Subjects: LCSH: International cooking. | LCGFT: Cookbooks.
    Classification: LCC TX725.A1 B524 2023 (print) | LCC TX725.A1 (ebook) |
        DDC 641.59—dc23/eng/20220806
    LC record available at https://lccn.loc.gov/2022034805
    LC ebook record available at https://lccn.loc.gov/2022034806

Hardcover ISBN: 978-1-9848-6056-9
eBook ISBN: 978-1-9848-6057-6

Printed in China

Editor-in-Chief: Bryant Terry | Creative Director: Amanda Yee
Acquiring editor: Kelly Snowden | Developmental editor: Emily Timberlake
Project editor: Claire Yee | Production editor: Ashley Pierce
Art director and designer: Betsy Stromberg | Production designer: Mari Gill
Cover designers: Sara Ridky and Betsy Stromberg | Chapter opener illustrator: Ohn Ho
Production manager: Serena Sigona | Prepress color manager: Jane Chinn
Recipe tester: Janelle Bitker | Food stylist: Lillian Kang | Food stylist assistant: Paige Arnett
Copyeditor: Shelley Berg | Proofreader: Allie Kiekhofer | Indexer: Eldes Tran
Publicist: Felix Cruz | Marketer: Joseph Lozada

10 9 8 7 6 5 4 3 2 1

First Edition